DATING
like
AIRPLANES

CALEB BREAKEY

HARVEST HOUSE PUBLISHERS
EUGENE, OREGON

Unless otherwise indicated, all Scripture quotations are from The ESV® Bible (The Holy Bible, English Standard Version®), copyright © 2001 by Crossway, a publishing ministry of Good News Publishers. Used by permission. All rights reserved.

Verses marked NIV are taken from the Holy Bible, New International Version®, NIV®. Copyright © 1973, 1978, 1984, 2011, by Biblica, Inc.™ Used by permission of Zondervan. All rights reserved worldwide. www.zondervan.com

Cover by Harvest House Publishers, Inc., Eugene, Oregon

Cover illustration © iStock / gavni

Back cover author photo by Carole Marie

Published in association with literary agent David Van Diest of D.C. Jacobson & Associates LLC, an Author Management Company. www.dcjacobson.com

DATING LIKE AIRPLANES

Copyright © 2014 by Caleb Jennings Breakey
Published by Harvest House Publishers
Eugene, Oregon 97402
www.harvesthousepublishers.com

Library of Congress Cataloging-in-Publication Data
    Breakey, Caleb Jennings, 1986-
    Dating like airplanes / Caleb Breakey.
        p. cm.
    Includes bibliographical references.
    ISBN 978-0-7369-5544-7 (pbk.)
    ISBN 978-0-7369-5545-4 (eBook)
    1. Man-woman relationships—Religious aspects—Christianity. 2. Dating (Social custom)—Religious aspects—Christianity. I. Title.
    BT705.8.B73 2013
    261.8'3573—dc23
                                                                2013030397

Printed in the United States of America

13 14 15 16 17 18 19 20 21 / BP-JH / 10 9 8 7 6 5 4 3 2 1

To Brittney, who got up and danced with me.

ACKNOWLEDGMENTS

To Buck, Beckie, Dave, and Shawn Marie, who set an example of unconditional love for Brittney and me.

To everyone who shared your ups and downs in learning to love.

To the incredible staff at Harvest House Publishers, whose passion for Christ shines through in first-rate work and warm smiles.

To my beautiful King, Jesus Christ, who gave me what I needed most.

CONTENTS

A NOTE FROM THE AUTHOR

*T*his isn't your typical foreword. My friend Brett Harris intended to write it, but he's busy loving and serving his bride, Ana, through a severe and complicated fight against Lyme disease. He's practicing the beautiful truth that exists at the center of all amazing relationships: *Giving your other what's needed most over taking what you want now.*

Brett wanted to write a foreword himself. He probably wanted to accomplish lots of good during these difficult days. But in true Jesus-love, he refuses to take what he wants now as he gives Ana what she needs most. Such love isn't easy. It takes selflessness, vulnerability, and a deep commitment to sacrificial love.

So whether you're years away from a relationship, invested in one right now, or feel as though you're too broken to ever try again, today is the day to rise to a love that's greater than yourself.

Today is the day to fly and not fall.

—Caleb Breakey for Brett Harris, co-author of Do Hard Things

Note: A portion of each purchase of *Dating Like Airplanes* will be donated to the Ana Harris fund and the fight against Lyme disease.

Part 1

FALLING IN LOVE

1

A BETTER WAY EXISTS

*In our love-hungry generation we struggle to believe
that the "beautiful side of love" really exists.*

ERIC AND LESLIE LUDY

Leaping into the Great Unknown

Something electric shocked my heart alive the day I first saw her.
I felt like I was standing under Niagara Falls. Or being shot into
a galaxy of new emotion. When Brittney swooped into my life, my
heart leaped into the great unknown of love—and I jumped in after it.

I knew that falling might mean pain. Maybe even a sort of emotional death if things didn't work out. But I also knew I couldn't just
stand at the precipice while my heart plunged into the mysterious
chasm below. Or so I thought.

I didn't know I had another option. I didn't know I could fly instead
of fall.

Eight years and one month after falling for Brittney, I kneeled on a
quiet riverbank, ring in hand. The look that lit her face was no different
from that on any other newly engaged woman. But in her eyes, I saw
so much more than thrill. I saw friendship and sacrificial love nurtured
since the day God snatched our falling relationship and—through the
good and bad—showed us the way of flying.

This book shows you a new way to do relationships. A way that
doesn't settle for true love's impostors, but chases after the Creator's love
that never, ever fails. Far-fetched? God only knows how many people
told me it was—and they'll tell you the same.

11

Don't listen.

You don't have to suffer unbearable confusion or break into a million pieces as you search for that special guy or girl to spend your life with. You can have peace and stay whole. And I'm not just talking about hiding in your Bible or abstaining from sex. Not at all.

If you want something you've never had, you must do something you've never done. If you want to transcend status quo relationships, you must fly and not fall.

That's what this book is about.

Flying vs. Falling

"Falling in love" is what it is—a very pleasant, very real brain obsession—but it's a dangerous and false god.

Gary Thomas[1]

When you fall, you're out of control. There's no slowing down. Nothing to hold on to. And no way to choose where you land—or crash. Gravity pulls you down, and your dominant thought is *Will I survive this?*

When you fly, you have stability. There's gliding and swooping. You're at once carefree and precise. Flying is graceful, swift, and efficient. And when gravity pulls you down, your prevalent thought is, *Where should I land?*

Flying still requires that you take a risk of the heart. But it's a risk entirely different from that of falling.

My hope is that by the time you finish the final chapter, you'll see the difference and choose to fly, not fall.

The Most Tragic Truth

Things that sound too good are usually a scam or only partly true.

So far, I've only told you half the truth about this new way of doing relationships. Because, honestly, the other half strikes most people as either trite or unhelpful, which is perhaps the most tragic oversight among frustrated singles today. So before I

Jesus lived and taught that friendship and love are marked by sacrifice.

Gary Thomas[2]

reveal the other half that makes flying possible, know that it contains the secret of true love. Because it does.

He does.

Jesus.

He is the one who makes you fly. The airplane that takes you into the great unknown with peace and strength. The power and presence you never thought possible.

> He can, without anything other than Himself, meet and overflow the deepest demands of our total nature, mysterious and deep as that nature is.
>
> A.W. Tozer[3]

I don't say this for the sake of a nice Christian visual. I say it because Jesus let me experience it in a very real way. That may not sound convincing now. But that's why the rest of the book exists.

Stay with me and you'll discover not only what Jesus wants to show you about flying with that special guy or girl, but also what he wants you to discover about *himself* that just might change how you do relationships—for now and for the rest of your life.

Who Should Read This Book

If you are one of the people described below, I believe this book will shape your love story in a beautiful way.

The *Leapers:* You have jumped into the great unknown of love... maybe more than once. You've suffered from relationships full of confusion and heartbreak. Sometimes you wonder if you're the problem. Other times you think the other person is to blame. Your feelings toward love have hardened since you first leaped. You've either cautiously withdrawn from it or you've continued to pursue a relationship but are now jaded or even a little cynical. Deep down, you long to experience a beautiful God-designed love. But the more you live, the more you wonder if such a love truly exists.

The *Ledgers:* You've walked up to the ledge of the great unknown many times. Your eyes are searching for someone you can spend the rest of your life with. Maybe you have someone in mind right now. It's not uncommon for you to daydream about what it will be like to love and be loved. Hearing of successful love stories encourages you that there's a way to fall in love without suffering the intense pain you've seen in other couples. But you wonder if it will ever happen to you. More than anything, you want to please God in your relationship with the opposite sex.

Flying doesn't come with any prerequisites. It doesn't matter if you've broken every relationship bone in your body or if you're emotionally whole. It doesn't matter if you've just started a relationship, have been in one for months, or are simply looking forward to one in the future.

All that matters is your willingness to rethink what true love looks like and start *living it*.

It's Not About What You Want

Falling in love is exhilarating—the rush of jumping off the ledge, the ecstasy of plunging into wide-open space—but it inevitably ends in broken bones. Not only your own, but also the bones of the one who has fallen with you.

Flying puts an end to that. Flying prevents brokenness.

> Over and over I have heard couples, including my own parents, say that their marriages only became great when they learned to give, love, and serve more than they sought to receive. This is a principle we can be practicing now.
>
> Rebecca St. James [4]

It's been said that discipline is choosing what you want most over what you want now. Combine this with one of the beautiful truths of Jesus—"It is more blessed to give than receive" (Acts 20:35)—and you will begin to see what it means to fly.

Flying is about giving your special other what he or she needs most instead of taking what you want now. This selfless act is the purest expression of love you could ever embrace. The wellspring from which marriage-ready relationships flow.

Now to clarify. The concept of flying is not based on the vague and frustrating Christian phrases you've heard before, such as:

- Don't give away your heart.
- Don't get into a relationship until you're (insert magical age).

- Don't go looking for that special someone—God will bring a spouse to you!

It's not that these sayings are all wrong. They're just not helpful. In the pages to come, my hope is that you'll discover that flying is so much more than a nice idea. It's about deeply loving Jesus and learning from him how to love your other. It's about preparing you for a lifetime of strong, powerful, three-corded love that saves you from the pain of falling.

Even the Sunk Can Soar

I learned about flying only after suffering my fair share of falling. It all started with the cutest thing I'd ever seen: Brittney Sue Jones.

> One of the great challenges of real love is the willingness to abandon your demand for a comfortable and predictable life.
>
> Paul David Tripp [5]

Brittney held my gaze from the moment she stepped into my church. Green eyes, adorable face, and a smile that glimmered like Christmas lights and church bells all at the same time—and I'm not even sure what that means.

Her hair kind of hid her eyes from the side, so she probably never noticed my jaw, which was not only on the floor, but halfway to the basement.

I was fourteen; she was eleven. Yeah.

I once daydreamed about the pastor—in mid-sermon—blurting out: "Contest for you singles: First person you hold hands with in the next ten seconds—you get to marry." I envisioned myself leaping pew over pew, bulldozing through every person who dared block my path.

When Brittney blipped onto my radar, every other girl blipped off. My mind connected every little thing in my day to her. She was my obsession. A stray wire sparking under my skin.

I set my heart on marrying her, and, to my surprise, she liked me back. And not only did she like me back. She made it known to lots of people that she liked me. This was like the prom queen falling for that guy over at the far table who I think I've seen before but I'm not sure and I guess it doesn't matter because he's a nobody. It was incredible.

- **Year one:** We talked, flirted, and liked each other more.

- **Year two:** Parents, friends, and everyone on the planet noticed us talking, flirting, and liking each other more.

- **Year three:** Everyone on the planet told us to stop liking each other because we were way too young.

- **Year four:** We got frustrated. Snuck around. Lied a lot. Got caught. Then the hammer fell.

"I love you, Caleb," I remember Brittney's father telling me. "But I don't trust you. There needs to be a separation between you and Britt."

Heartbroken, I asked, "How long?"

"I don't know. Could be two months, could be two years."

Turned out to be longer than both of those combined—no communication allowed. Not a call, not a whisper.

My world crumbled after my cutoff from Brittney. But nobody knew. I kept my hurt and longing inside, distracting myself with friends and nonstop activity. When everyone left, I'd either go to my room or pull over my car—and cry.

Every week I saw her talking with other people. Heard how her family spent a lot of time with families with guys her age.

Wondering. Questioning.

A time of profound loneliness, pain, and inner rebellion followed. I wanted to take what I wanted now (Brittney's affection) instead of giving her what she needed most: space for both of us to grow up and learn the way of Jesus.

Thankfully, the story doesn't end there. Jesus turned me around and helped me do some things right. Like loving only one girl, buying only one ring, and saving my virginity for one person.

Now I've been married to Brittney long enough to count our anniversaries on two hands. And I'm not going to hold back in describing what flying during our relationship eventually meant for our marriage. It's been amazing. Ridiculous. *Blessed.*

More and more, Brittney chooses to give me the true love I need most. And thanks to Jesus, I cannot help but reciprocate with all of my heart.

This is flying. This is what we'll explore throughout this book.

A Better Way Exists

A strange phenomenon occurred when I transitioned from my teens to my twenties. Every time I entered a room full of people, a sense of longing overcame me. It took almost two years to understand why.

God had put a desire in me to give to others instead of take. He wanted me to touch lives, not just talk about sports or the latest viral video. This meant doing the harder thing. Looking out for the needs and hurts of others. Living intentionally. And in doing so, I truly started living.

A better way existed. The way of Jesus.

> "This is my commandment, that you love one another as I have loved you" (John 15:12).

Jesus loved us by sacrificing himself and giving us intimacy with God instead of handing us over to our own desires for sin and separation. He gave us what we needed most instead of what we wanted now. He alone made it possible to fly and not fall.

If you're a Leaper or Ledger, then you're on the verge of a spectacular battle. *Spectacular* because flying is unlike anything you've ever experienced. *Battle* because you've got to fight to fly and not fall.

A relationship, by its very definition, can't be found; it has to be built.

Gary Thomas[6]

You ready? If you dig deep and stay true to the principles in this book, you'll experience less hurt, more beauty, and a soaring kind of love that everyone wants but too few choose. Sound good?

Welcome to an electrifying time of life.

2

TO THE WOUNDED AND THE TENACIOUS

To the Wounded

*I*f you're thinking to yourself, *I've screwed up way too much to ever do this flying thing*, please stop.

The past is the past. Your new start begins now.

It hurts to bring up past sin and failure with the next person you begin a relationship with. It may even be too much for the other person to handle. And that hurts. It makes you want to bury your past deep in your soul and never speak of it again.

Don't succumb to that. What's happened in your past has happened. You may not be proud of it, but now isn't the time to hide what you're ashamed of. It's time to let your mistakes shape who you are today.

Don't let your past consume you. Instead throw yourself on Jesus, shower in his grace, and move on practicing the love of Christ.

God uses the weak, not the strong; the broken, not the whole. Just look to Scripture: Paul committed multiple murders. Joseph suffered physical and mental abuse. Samson womanized. Rahab slept around. Elijah entertained suicide. Jonah ran from God. Jacob lied.

Your past doesn't disqualify you. If anything, it makes you more prepared to be used for him. That doesn't mean you should aspire to sin more. It simply means you're never too far gone.

Regret and remorse are going to try to make you feel like you've blown your chance at a beautiful romance.

You haven't, friend.

You'll have unique challenges and struggles to face, but we all do. The fact that you must tell your next boyfriend or girlfriend that you've slept with someone isn't all that different from a virgin who is chained by pornography, lies, or a lukewarm relationship with Jesus. All of these sins will hurt you and your other to a greater or lesser degree. All of these sins will play a part in whether or not the two of you move forward in the relationship.

But they do not end God's amazing ability to bring two messed up people together and make a beautiful relationship that pleases him until death do you part.

You are a new person in Christ. Your sins are nailed to the cross, and when God looks at you, he doesn't see how many people you've given yourself to. He sees Jesus.

So confess your sins to God, own up to your past, and let his beautiful grace empower you to start giving your other what he or she needs most instead of taking what you want now.

> But he said to me, "My grace is sufficient for you, for my power is made perfect in weakness." Therefore I will boast all the more gladly of my weaknesses, so that the power of Christ may rest upon me (2 Corinthians 12:9).

To the Tenacious

Chances are that you've seen or read J.R.R. Tolkien's The Lord of the Rings series—or at the very least heard of it. Laced throughout this fictional masterpiece is the character Gollum, a creature transformed and corrupted by the powerful ring, which Gollum refers to as "my precious."

Hidden within Gollum's story is a truth you need to consider.

Gollum so loved the ring—his precious—that the peripherals of everything else happening around him faded into oblivion. Nothing captures this better than one of the final scenes in the final part of the trilogy, The Return of the King.

Finally taking the ring on the edge of Mount Doom, Gollum falls to his death with the ring in hand. In those few moments, the reality that his life is over doesn't even cross his mind. He's too consumed with his precious. Only in the final moment of his life does he realize his plight. Then he's gone forever.

Before we move forward, it's imperative that you don't let the idea of flying consume you to the point that it destroys you. Let me explain.

Some people really like to go all-in. I'm one of them. When I truly believe in something, I pour my everything into it. This can lead to great things. I pursued Brittney for eight years, and finally put a ring on her finger. I sent out nearly a hundred applications all over the country looking for writing internships, and finally got one with mlb.com covering the New York Yankees.

But other times, tenacity and an all-in attitude can really hurt you. Because giving everything you've got to something can transform you into a Gollum. You get so obsessed that you lose sight of what's good for you and what isn't.

Going into your relationship determined to give your other what he or she needs most can transform into ugly things like trying to control your other, as if you know what's best for him or her in *everything*—not just the Jesus-focused principles outlined in this book.

Likewise, refusing to take what you want now can morph into ugly things like censoring your wants so severely that you leave no room to be a contributor to the relationship and steal joy from your other.

What starts as a loving thing twists into a horrible thing. Don't let that happen in your current or future relationship. Always remember that flying will only ever be as amazing as your ability to pursue it in a way that stays true to the way of Jesus.

3

WHY YOU SHOULD FLY

Avoiding dating isn't the way to cure problems encountered in dating. The cure is the same as the Bible's cure for all life's problems, and that is spiritual growth leading to maturity.

HENRY CLOUD AND JOHN TOWNSEND

replayed the message, heart thumping and mind reeling. I remember thinking to myself, *Did I really just hear her say that?*

"Okay, I love you," Brittney said at the end of her voicemail, almost nonchalantly. I listened to those words over and over while lying on my back in my bedroom. Few moments compete with the raw emotion that rushed through me that first time Brittney told me she loved me.

But twenty minutes away, in a little Pacific Northwest town, Brittney was filling in the first page of another journal. She wrote, "This journal is about a girl who is in sin. Please do not become like her. Your life will be sad, depressing, burdensome, scary, dreadfully hard, and lots, lots more."

How could such soul torment and beautiful emotion coexist in our relationship? It's actually not complicated.

We were in *love*. We were *falling*.

This chapter unveils the way of flying, and shows you why it's so important not only to your future, but to the core of who you are. That said, the following is no bed of roses. There's nothing simple, formulaic, or less painful about choosing flying over falling. It's just better.

Much better.

What You've Always Wanted Most

Step into the sandals of the eleven remaining disciples the day Jesus carried the cross to Golgotha. Imagine peeling back their skin and seeing straight into their souls.

Horror. Anguish. Nothing but darkness. More than anything, they wanted Jesus to drop the cross, part the crowd, and return to them. They didn't realize the magnitude of what Christ was about to accomplish. They didn't know that getting what they wanted then would've cost them what they needed most: a Savior to die for their sin.

Falling *wants*—and usually with good intention. It wants the other's attention, it wants their affection, it wants their time. Not some of it. Not part of it. Falling in love just *wants*. And that's the problem. It doesn't stop wanting until it ruins whatever was good about the relationship in the first place.

Flying, on the other hand, gives. It gives attention, it gives affection, it gives time. And it gives what's needed most: Jesus's love.

And it doesn't stop. Ever.

If you desire a relationship that binds you to your other and moves toward fully enjoying the brilliance of marriage, then it's time to do the hard thing. The temporary difficulty of flying pales in comparison to the lifelong heartache of falling.

> This is how we know what love is: Jesus Christ laid down his life for us. And we ought to lay down our lives for our brothers and sisters (1 John 3:16 NIV).

What the Bible Says About Relationships

Early in my relationship with Brittney, I felt like burying my face in the sand. Not because we'd done something wrong, but because neither of us knew what to do *right*. We were subtly directed not to talk with each other until we were older, but nothing else. We were given a list of "thou shalt nots" but no direction about doing relationships right. This led both of us into emotional tailspins.

There's much more to the story, but the takeaway is this: We needed someone to go to Scripture and show us what God says about relationships.

Obviously there's no Book of Relationships in the Bible, but there are so many beautiful truths that show us how to date well. Like giving what's needed most over taking what's wanted now. This kind of Jesus love gets to know the other in a way that's so far beyond physical attraction (Proverbs 19:2). It goes above and beyond in showing honor (Romans 12:10). It radiates patience, kindness, and truthfulness to the other, always doing what lifts up (1 Corinthians 13:4-7). It clothes itself in humility and makes itself a servant to helping the other progress in character (1 Peter 5:5).

It builds respect by treating the other as though he or she were a brother or sister—and the very temple of God (1 Corinthians 3:16-17). It speaks to the other with integrity and dignity (Titus 2:7-8) and refuses to lust with its eyes (Matthew 5:27-30). It does everything it possibly can to keep the other sexually pure and emotionally whole, even if it means seeking help outside of the relationship (1 Corinthians 6:18; Proverbs 4:23; Proverbs 15:22; Proverbs 27:12). It cries out for God to search itself for mixed motives and manipulative ways (Psalm 139:23-24). It always plans ahead, knowing that it wants to do what's right but far too easily chooses what's wrong instead (Matthew 26:41).

Above all, it ignites a beautiful romance by helping the other seek God first in everything (Proverbs 16:3; Matthew 6:33). It sets its mind to helping the other lay up treasures in heaven, live by every word of God, and exude intimacy with Jesus (Matthew 6:19; Matthew 4:4). It challenges the other to dive deeper into the abundance of Christ, gaze at his beauty, dwell on his loving-kindness, and praise him for all that he's done (Psalm 27:4; Isaiah 63:7).

> Values are part of your life. Forge them out of what the Bible teaches. Make them part of your dating world.
>
> Henry Cloud and
> John Townsend[1]

The statements above probably feel overwhelming—too much for any one person to handle. They might make you think, *So all I have to do is be perfect? Great. Thanks for that.*

The fact is, yes, flying requires a lot. And if this book were based merely on *dos* and *do nots*, it would be impossible.

But it's not. It's based on Jesus.

Not the safe, Christianized Jesus many of us take him to be. I'm talking about the Jesus who wants a thriving, growing, supernatural relationship with you. The Jesus who says you will do greater things than he, becoming witnesses to the entire world through the Holy Spirit (John 14:12). The Jesus who's waiting for you to move mountains, walk on water, stun religious people, and turn this world upside-down.

Knowing and following this Jesus is the basis of flying. It's the prerequisite to everything in the chapters to come. If this intrigues you, the best is yet to come.

Why You Should Fly

Flying teaches you how to give instead of take. It pushes you to become the love-filled, others-focused person God created you to be. It unveils the somewhat paradoxical truth that to love someone completely, you must first completely love Jesus.

It also helps you decide things like: When is the right time for a relationship? Should I search for someone or wait?

> The world's view about relationships and marriage is all about "me, myself, and I." It feeds us a user mentality that says "If he pleases me, then I'll stay with him," or "If she serves me as she should, then we'll stick together." It is about conditional commitment and, ultimately, complete selfishness.
>
> Rebecca St. James[2]

What should I look for in the other person? How should I present myself? What are the most important things I can do to show the love of Jesus to my other? What kind of dangers should I watch for?

Flying doesn't avoid hurt, frustration, or disappointment. Nothing ever avoids these aspects of life. Instead it comes out of the fire refined into something better than it was before.

In other words, whether things go easy or rough in your relationship, flying leads you to know a deeper, greater love.

This is the most astounding difference between flying and falling.

Flying meets difficulty and says, "I will love because Jesus first loved me." But falling meets difficulty and says, "We were never meant to be."

This is why breakups and divorces run rampant. People expect perfection, not imperfection. They want the other's love, but not the problems.

Flying gives love despite the other's problems. It expects imperfection because it intimately knows its own imperfections.

That may not sound incredibly romantic now. But it's true of all incredible romances.

When You Choose to Fly...
You Go into the Relationship with Purpose

To date without the end goal of marriage is the exact opposite of giving someone what he or she needs most. It takes what you want and ultimately leaves the other hurt and broken. Your other needs to know that you are dating him or her to gauge whether or not forever makes sense for both of you.

> The goal of Christian dating is not to have a boyfriend or girlfriend but to find a spouse. Have that in mind as you get to know one another, and if you're not ready to commit to a relationship with the end goal of marriage, it's better not to date but simply to remain friends.
>
> Mark Driscoll[3]

So before you even begin your relationship, ask yourself: *Is this someone I could spend my life with?*

I'm not saying you have to come out and say *I'm lookin' to marry you, sweet thang* on a first date. I'm just saying that, before long, you need to be perfectly clear about your intentions.

I like how my friend Jefferson Bethke, author of *Jesus>Religion* puts it: Dating without marriage in mind is like walking into a store with no money—you'll either leave hungry or take something that doesn't belong to you.

No marriage equals no purpose. And no purpose equals no point.

You Become Who You Are Meant to Be

It's been said that you only make three or four big decisions in life. To fly or fall is one of them, along with choosing to become a completely committed follower of Jesus, picking a career that empowers your passions and gifts, and, of course, saying "I do."

Choosing to fly isn't about trying out a new way to date. It's about loving Jesus. It's about living your life as he's told you to live.

If you feel as though you can skip sections like this because you already believe in Jesus, you're missing the point of what's going to transform the way you do relationships. Trying to build an intimate, satisfying relationship with a special other without having an intimate, satisfying relationship with Christ—beyond just belief—is like trying to land on the moon without NASA.

This is why flying requires that you dive deeply into who you are and get honest about what you find.

> The man who has God for his treasure has all things in One...Whatever he may lose he has actually lost nothing, for he now has it all in One, and he has it purely, legitimately and forever.
>
> A.W. Tozer[4]

Unless you can tell Jesus Christ that you love him more than anything or anyone and live a life that reflects it from the core of your being, you'll be flying a plane without wings. I'm not advocating learning how to say the right things and do the right things. That's just dead religion. I'm challenging you to open your heart to Jesus and to let him dwell not only in the places where you feel comfortable with him, but also in the places you've consciously or subconsciously reserved for only you.

This complete indwelling makes flying possible. In ways you cannot fathom, Jesus helps you exchange your selfishness with his selflessness, your impatience with his patience, your harshness with his gentleness, your deceit with his truthfulness, your negativity with his hopefulness, your boastfulness with his humility, your worthless talk with his meaningful words, your manipulation with his honesty, and your spiritual laziness with his spiritual zeal.

Flying isn't about becoming perfect. It's about giving Jesus total access to your imperfections—areas he wants to redeem and take up residence in. In that sense, flying begins at the end of yourself. When you allow Jesus in, you discover a supernatural power that replaces

> The more our lives are surrendered to him, the more he is able to fashion our lives as we were meant to be.
>
> Henry Cloud and John Townsend[5]

everything you've ever hated about yourself with a deep love for God, which radiates love to others. You find your truest identity. You discover exactly who you are meant to be: a person capable of loving others as Christ loved you.

You Practice the Golden Rule

How the Golden Rule ever got its name, I have no idea. A more straightforward moniker would be the Hypocrisy Detector. Because that's exactly what it does. It detects what you really want for yourself but are not eager to give to another.

> There is no way to escape it—real love is costly. Real love calls each of us to be willing to suffer.
>
> Paul David Tripp[6]

Answer the following questions to detect hypocrisy in yourself:

- Would you want your other judging you first and foremost by your physical attributes?
- Would you want your other judging you for the things in your past?
- Would you want your other telling you what you want to hear instead of the truth?
- Would you want your other getting intimate with another person?
- Would you want your other to pressure you into making a commitment before you're ready?
- Would you want your other acting as if he or she had it all together in life?
- Would you want your other lusting after others or mired in pornography?
- Would you want someone to sexually seduce your other or play with his or her emotions?
- Would you want your other to not care about your relationship with Jesus?

- Would you want your other to make you think more of this life and little of heaven?

- Would you want your other to hinder you from seeking God first in everything?

- Would you want your other always relying on you to be the spiritually strong one?

- Would you want your other to speak little of the things of God or to pray sparingly?

> To get to this place, we literally have to declare spiritual war against our selfishness.
>
> Gary Thomas[7]

- Would you want your other to always choose what was best for him or her—instead of you?

- Would you want your other to pursue a relationship without the intention of marrying you?

- Would you like it if your other showed little interest in your interests?

To crush hypocrisy, you must stop judging the other's past. Stop just saying whatever you think he or she wants to hear. Stop trying to seduce, get physical with, or toy with the other's emotions. Stop rushing the relationship. Stop trying to appear flawless. Stop lusting after them, fantasizing about them, or indulging yourself in pornography.

> [Your other's] needs above your own for the rest of your life—regardless of what happens. Are you ready for that?
>
> Gary Thomas[8]

And start caring about the other's relationship with Jesus. Start making a bigger deal of heaven. And, above all, start helping them seek God in *everything*.

Most of us interpret the Golden Rule as doing things that make the other feel good. But that's not accurate. If it were, we'd simply say whatever made the other smile, do whatever turned them on, and make them think we were the best thing that had ever happened to them.

But the Golden Rule isn't about making another feel good. It's about looking at your own hypocrisy in order to help you choose what's best for your other—and ultimately you. Think of all the intangibles you wish your other would one day be to you (i.e. loving, pure, selfless). Then be those things to him or her. Think of all the intangibles you wish your other *wouldn't* be to you. Then resolve not to be those things to him or her.

We are not the exception to our own standards. Instead, we should make ourselves servants to living out our standards to our others.

> So in everything, do to others what you would have them do to you, for this sums up the Law and the Prophets (Matthew 7:12 NIV).

You Free Others to Fly

There's a brilliant video on YouTube that takes place at a music festival called Sasquatch in my home state of Washington. The clip starts out with two guys dancing like amateurs alongside a hill away from the main crowd, just having a good time. Within seconds, a third dancer joins. Then a fourth and fifth. And a minute later the entire Gorge is dancing.

In the most unusual way, the two friends learned a simple but profound truth: It only takes two to start something amazing.

So it is with flying.

When it comes to relationships, most of us are lounging on the hill with the crowd instead of getting in on the real fun. We do this because it's the way we've learned and observed. We do this because trying something different, especially something that so few are doing, scares us.

To fly is to dance.

People think you're weird at first. They ask you questions and sometimes mock your responses. If I received a #CalebIsDumb for every time someone told me Brittney and I were crazy for waiting for each other, for not trying out other people before marriage, I'd still be trending.

But when all is said and done, the ones who dare to do relationships differently are the ones who experience true love.

It's almost sad to see people from my past who obnoxiously spoke against my relationship with Brittney. There's so much hurt in their eyes now. So much brokenness. Then when they see that I'm married to *that girl*, it's like salt on an open wound. I hate it. But it's reality.

You can choose to be like everyone else and laugh at the dancers, which might feel good in the moment. But one day the regret will hit, and it will hit hard. Be different. Stop sitting on the hill. Do the crazy thing. Get up and let the rest of the world think you're nuts. They won't for long. And some will even join you.

You Strategize for Success

Say you and your other are going to enjoy a picnic at the park. Most people think, *show up, eat, and have a good time*. But the intentional love of flying goes deeper:

Those who fly think of questions that might help the two of you get to know each other intellectually, emotionally, and spiritually. They consider how to make the other feel comfortable—something as simple as parking in a visible place, setting up the blanket in the safest and most relaxed location, or turning off their phone.

They remember the conversation topics that are important to the other, and make them the priority in the conversation.

They consider the negative vibes that have crept up in the relationship—perhaps flirting gone too far, too much useless talk, or looking at the other in a way you shouldn't—and plan on avoiding them. They consider their motives, asking: *Why am I doing what I'm doing? Is it because I want my other to think I'm amazing? Or because I truly want the best for him or her?*

Above all, they wonder how to give their other Jesus. Perhaps this means getting vulnerable about their relationship with Christ. Or talking about where they've seen God in their life this past week, or where he's seemed absent. Or asking the other to pray for them in specific areas, or how they can pray for the other.

One clarification. Though intentional love is intensely focused, it shouldn't be forced. The point isn't to go into a date with a mental list of things to say and do. The point is to have thought about what you might say and do so that you can react to situations organically. So keep this idea in mind:

Think hard before. React easy later.

You Pour the Foundation for the Spectacular

Relationships should be spectacular. Relationships should be fun. Relationships should be filled with love, laughter, unity, and pleasure. But the truth is that not everyone who flies will experience this kind of joy. This is why it's important to know what traits to look for in your other.

There are three ways a flying relationship can function:

1. **Only one of you flies.** The best relationship starts with choosing what your other needs most over what you want now. This Jesus-powered change alone will transform who you are, how you live, and the way you do relationships. Yet at the end of the day, if you keep dating people who don't want to fly with you, the relationship might work but it won't ever be spectacular.

2. **Both of you fly.** If you put your other's needs above your wants *and* your other reciprocates, you'll experience an extraordinary relationship. You will both become a microcosm of true love. It's hard to imagine a relationship like this ever falling apart. But just because something doesn't fall apart doesn't mean it's spectacular. It just means it's steady and secure. What's spectacular is when steady and secure meets fun and friendship.

3. **Both of you fly and share common interests, goals, and values.** This final tier of flying is something we've yet to discuss: The tier of common interests, compatible goals, and similar values. I know the words *interests*, *goals*, and

values don't sound very spectacular. But like wind under wings, they are vital in turning a gentle glide into an astounding airshow.

A good way to gauge whether the two of you share this third tier is by asking yourselves these questions:

- **Interests:** Do you enjoy doing similar activities in your spare time?

- **Goals:** Are your passions and desires to contribute to the world complementary in some way?

- **Values:** Do your convictions push you toward greater respect and unity with each other, or anger and detachment?

Growing in unison in these three areas of life can ignite a holy infatuation. Common interests, goals, and values magnetize you to your other in a way that lasts a lifetime instead of just two years (which researchers claim is the lifespan of infatuation). I'm not talking about idolizing each other. I'm simply talking about enjoying the beauty of a complementary relationship and lifestyle. I love waking up and staring at Brittney as she sleeps, wanting her to wake up so we can talk and laugh and attack the day together.

> Holding people up to unrealistic expectations will only result in frustration on your part and the part of those who wish to pursue you, and may cause you to miss out on a great potential mate.
>
> Mark Driscoll[9]

But let me say this again: Interests, goals, and values are not the foundation of flying. They simply make the flight more enjoyable.

Don't get too nit-picky here. Don't start overlooking people as potential spouses simply because they don't like cars, or jogging, or whatever. Don't go looking for someone who lines up with you on every interest, goal, and value. That's a great way to stay single forever.

Just be aware.

Know that a lifetime of doing the same things during your spare time means something to your relationship. Know that the depth of your conversations will be sweeter when your passions and desires complement one another. Know that unity in your values will spare you from what could later be severe sparks.

Till death do us part is a long time. What better way to spend your lifetime than with a best friend who's in tune with your interests, goals, and values?

You Embrace True Love Instead of Its Impostors

Complaining about the nonexistence of true love has almost become as cliché as dreamily talking about happily ever after. Lasting love does exist. The problem is that too few can distinguish it from its impostors.

Flying helps you do just that.

Impostors of true love aren't all bad. They just have a bad habit of wearing a label that doesn't belong to them. You probably recognize these common pretenders as:

> A lot of counterfeit loves lurk out there. After all, just as you have a Hero fervently seeking your heart, a Villain is eager to stomp on your soul. He will stop at nothing to see the picture of God's great love destroyed in your life.
>
> Dannah Gresh[10]

Infatuation: *I can't stop thinking about you and my heart beats wildly every time I'm around you.* Infatuation is a natural thing. The problem is that it's like a drug that numbs you to reality. Infatuation gets mistaken for true love more than any other imposter because of its powerful pull on the heart. But studies show infatuation wanes after a couple of years. It's not true love.

Compatibility: *We like all of the same things, believe all of the same things, and want to accomplish all of the same things. It's so easy to talk to each other and nothing is ever awkward.* Compatibility is another very good thing. Who doesn't want to be in a relationship with a best friend? But no two human beings are perfectly compatible. Eventually we argue, get on each other's nerves, or disappoint each other. When this happens, compatibility falls apart. It's not true love.

Adaptation: *I'm willing to do anything, say anything, or become* *anything to be with this person.* Adaptation is tricky because it can disguise itself as sacrifice. But at its core, adaptation isn't sacrifice at all. Adaptation says, "I will do whatever it takes to become the person my other wants me to be." Sacrifice says, "I will do whatever it takes to be like Jesus to my other." Adaptation is not true love.

Attraction: *I'm dead gone on how amazing my other looks.* If you're resisting the urge to lust, attraction is great. But attraction is not true love. It shouldn't be disregarded in the relationship, but it shouldn't be the basis either. Sooner or later, physical beauty and fitness wane. Attraction is a wonderful thing and you should be attracted to the person you're in a relationship with. But attraction alone is not true love.

True love starts at giving what's needed most over taking what's wanted now. From there, infatuation can be amazing. Compatibility rocks. And attraction intensifies. So build your relationship on Jesus and loving sacrifice. Only then will you see impostors as decorations instead of foundations.

You Retain a Most Valuable Commodity

Our individual sins reap consequences—some more than others. And getting intimate with someone before marriage is no exception.

If you've already fooled around, reread chapter 2. You are just as whole as anyone who is swimming in the grace of Jesus. You'll have to face difficult conversations with your other about your past, but you are not alone.

Start choosing the way of our amazing Creator, which is purity until marriage (Hebrews 13:4). He knows what he's doing. God doesn't want you to wait so that your hormones explode. He wants you to wait because anything else robs you of the most intimate blessings you can share with your other (more on this in chapter 6).

Be the one who keeps your body unscathed and you will be one of the rarest commodities on earth—and your other will respect you like crazy for it.

> Flee from sexual immorality. Every other sin a person commits is outside the body, but the sexually immoral person sins against his own body (1 Corinthians 6:18).

You Gain Trust and Respect from Your Other

Sometimes you don't value what you have until you lose it. This was my case with trust and respect. I'll never forget the day Brittney's father looked me in the eyes and said, "I love you, Caleb, but I don't trust you." That cut my soul. I lost something extremely valuable that day—something I couldn't just fix.

Flying builds trust and respect because you're looking out for your other's spiritual, emotional, and physical needs: what they need from you, and what they need you to restrain yourself from.

> Love waits to give, but lust can't wait to get.
>
> Henry Cloud
> and John Townsend[11]

Most people believe this starts when they enter a relationship. That's a big, big lie.

Trust and respect starts now, this very moment.

- You can stop focusing so much on people's outsides and start focusing on the heart.

- You can start loving people no matter what they've done instead of holding grudges against fellow sinners.

- You can work on speaking the truth in love instead of just saying what you think others want to hear.

- You can practice discernment, learning what is non-negotiable about the Bible, what the gray areas are, and what is not biblical.

- You can start getting vulnerable with people, not being ashamed of the unique struggles you face.

- You can put an end to lust, purging your life of everything that makes you fall—even if it seems impractical.

- You can care so much about your relationship with Jesus that all other relationships come in a far second.

- You can learn the art of living life with heaven in mind, flushing your mind of the American Dream mentality.

- You can do everything you possibly can to be the best man or woman you could ever be for your special other.

- And, more than anything, you can pour your life into loving God with all of your heart, mind, soul, and strength—
  and others as yourself.

That starts now. Every decision you make either builds a runway for your relationship to take off from or digs a pit.

Start choosing the runway.

> Do not be deceived: God is not mocked, for whatever one
> sows, that will he also reap. For the one who sows to his
> own flesh will from the flesh reap corruption, but the one
> who sows to the Spirit will from the Spirit reap eternal life
> (Galatians 6:7-8).

You Focus on the Line, Not the Dot

Author Randy Alcorn talks about the line and the dot in life—the dot representing our temporary lives on earth, and the line represent- ing our eternal lives in heaven.

This is a great metaphor for relationships.

> Marriage isn't about being young together; it's about growing old together.
>
> Gary Thomas[12]

To enter the dating world wanting, wanting, and wanting is to focus on the dot. You will get some temporary plea- sure in dating around and flirting, but you'll be missing out on so much more.

When you give, give, give, you dis- cover what it means to live life with intense affection for your other. Not just physically, but emotionally and spiritually. Not just for a year or two, but until death separates you.

When you're giving and watching everyone else taking, you might be tempted to think that everyone else seems happy and you're miss- ing out on something.

Trust me, you're not.

You may see smiles on the outsides, but there's far more hurt and insecurity happening on the insides.

Living for the line stores up everything you seem to be missing out on in the dot—then explodes into a lifetime of something better. Real love. Real commitment. Real security. There's simply no comparison between the two. Taking usually feels like the right thing to do in the moment, but it always ends the same: Brokenness. Live for the line, not the dot.

You Take Risks in a Safer Way

Getting involved romantically with anyone—and pretty much at any stage—is a risk. You put yourself out there. You say, *Here I am, and there you are: Do you think we could live and laugh and love forever?* That's vulnerable.

When someone says *no* at any point in the relationship, you're going to feel rejected. You're going to feel like something is wrong with you. Flying helps you take the risk of love in a way that protects your soul. It keeps you from having to face the dark rejection that comes with being sent away by someone you've shared your body with or idolized as the center of your identity—both of which happen regularly in falling relationships.

This kind of pain is hard to recover from. If not emotionally, then physically. And if not physically, then spiritually. It cuts deep and leaves scars that do not go away easily.

Breakups still happen in flying relationships, for sure. But separating from someone because it just doesn't seem to be working out versus separating from someone after you've allowed him or her into a sacred part of your soul where only Jesus belongs are two different things.

If your relationship ever reaches the point of breakup, it's going to hurt. But with flying, when Jesus alone gives you your identity, the pain is far less and the comfort far more.

You Become a Part of the Solution

It's no secret that the way most people do relationships is messed up. We as a country didn't get a ginormous divorce rate by accident. We worked up to it by the acceptance of shallow commitment, selfish ambition, and separation as the logical fix.

Flying takes a jackhammer to this messed-up foundation and

rebuilds something much stronger. It looks at the monstrosity of what our culture settles for and says, *No. I'll risk building something new rather than living in that unstable scrapheap.* It dares to imagine something better.

Why should you accept the broken way of this world? Why should you enter a dangerous building hoping against hope that you and your other will somehow be the exception and survive? Why not exchange the pain of what normalcy offers for the thrill of blazing your own path?

That's flying.

Some might criticize you. Some might get jealous that you braved the unknown and escaped normalcy. But all will watch you because they're curious to see the result.

Show the world that there's a way of less pain, more joy, and a kind of love that never, ever fails.

The way of Jesus.

You Embrace That You Are Not Your Own

Take a minute to think about a time when you poured your heart and soul into a person you love only to watch him or her not give a care. It hurts. It cuts deep. You feel like no matter how much you care for the other, he or she will never feel it. And, ultimately, you feel useless and betrayed.

> If you have decent families, honor them. Allow them to speak into your relationship and know the person you are considering.
>
> Mark Driscoll[13]

This is how we make loved ones feel when we fall and break.

Our lives may be our own—but not completely. We are each a product first of God's handiwork and second of those who've loved us and helped us reach this point in our lives. Flying embraces these truths by doing relationships in a way that doesn't open itself to the broken bones of falling. It puts others at ease the same way a parent is at ease knowing that their son or daughter is driving with a seatbelt on.

A lot of us go against the advice of our parents to prove a point. Then, like a blade, that point ends up stabbing us deep. Not everyone who gives you advice actually gives good advice—some parents included. But you become stronger when you let the people who love you most speak into your dating relationship. Where you are blind, they help you see. Where you are weak, they strengthen you. Where you are deaf, they hear.

People who truly love you are not out to steal your joy or undermine your relationship. They simply want to see their investment in you flourish.

> "Honor your father and mother" (this is the first commandment with a promise), "that it may go well with you and that you may live long in the land" (Ephesians 6:2-3).

Profile of a Flyer

Those who fly give the other what he or she needs most instead of taking what they want now. They replace selfish motives and desires with the beautiful, simple call of Christ.

Those who fly don't look for someone who is perfect. They look to become the person Jesus calls them to be. They don't force convictions on the other. They look to help the other embrace the convictions of Christ. They desperately want the other to love God abundantly more than them.

> The most accurate definition of true love is found in John 15:13: 'Greater love has no one than this, that he lay down his life for his friends.' This love isn't based on feelings; it's based on sacrifice.
>
> Gary Thomas[14]

Those who fly know they cannot give what they do not have. They're acutely aware that unless the Holy Spirit is thriving inside, they won't be in a position to give someone what he or she needs most. Their first priority and most important relationship is with Jesus.

Those who fly eagerly seek out the knowledge of those with mature relationships. They learn from the mistakes of others, ask for help when they need assistance, accountability when they need support, advice when they need direction, and honesty when they need the truth.

Those who fly don't give what's best to gain favor with God. They give what's best because God's shown them that living out sacrificial love is the ultimate kind of relationship two people can share. They don't feel entitled to an easier life by doing the hard thing of flying.

They simply do so because they want to follow the beautiful way of Jesus.

The Three Ways of a Flyer
Selflessness

Ask yourself how Jesus would love your other. Ask yourself what you expect but do not want to give. Expect less and give more. Ask yourself what things you may be doing that are distancing your other from God. Ask yourself what things you may have overlooked that might benefit him or her.

Ask how you can best pray for your other, and do it fervently. Consider how you can best lead conversations that celebrate the Creator of love more than just love itself. Keep yourself from becoming an idol to your other. Think about how you can protect him or her from choosing anything less than Jesus.

Become a student of your other. Learn to love in ways that make him or her feel most loved, always pointing to Jesus. Consider what future regrets they may have if the relationship doesn't work out, and do whatever you can to quell those possible regrets.

Think about what your other may be wondering about you at any given moment. Consider their thoughts, concerns, and curiosities, and do your best to open yourself up so that they're not left wanting or wondering. Go out of your way to make him or her feel safe, loved, and cared for.

Express genuine interest in your other's interests. Step into their shoes and imagine if their interests, goals, and values were your own. Try to think as your other thinks and practice empathy.

Encourage your other with Scripture. Extend love to his or her friends and family. Protect their physical, emotional, and spiritual states at all times. And consider how to express that marriage is your goal without scaring him or her off before they really know you.

> Let each of you look not only to his own interests, but also
> to the interests of others (Philippians 2:4).

Vulnerability

Speak in a way that is both truthful and fits the occasion. Dive into the harder topics of conversation when appropriate. Discuss your relationship with Jesus, your shortcomings as a person, and the battles that go on within you.

Consider how you can paint a picture of who you are. Let your other know your past, present, and plans for the future. Be open about your quirks and inconsistencies. Be transparent about the things you're passionate about and aspire to. Discuss the questions you have about God, the Bible, and following Jesus.

Hang out with each other in different situations. Don't just do dinner and candlelight. Do homemade pizza and porch swings. Throw a football around. Talk around a dinner table with family and with friends. Try working together, serving together, and just having fun together and being goofy. Try your hand at each other's interests. Invest yourself in understanding what makes the other tick.

Be attentive not only to what the other person is saying with his or her mouth, but also their body language. Look for opportunities to help him or her become more vulnerable and authentic. Help your other see that the best way to go where Jesus wants all of us to go—to himself—begins with vulnerability.

Transcendence

Fix your eyes on the transcendent plan God has for relationships and ultimately marriage. Consider what the Bible says they mirror. Rise to the occasion of self-sacrifice because Jesus did so for us undeserving sinners. Rise to the occasion of being humble and vulnerable like our King.

Jesus is coming back to make his bride beautiful and spend forever and ever with her. Keep your eyes on the end example of Christ and his bride. Know that you are a child of the King and don't have any part in the way the world does relationships. Know that your Creator spun something so much better and wants you to want it for yourself as badly as he wants it for you.

Treat your relationships the same way you treat your worship. Approach the quest for companionship as sweet and sacred. Picture being baptized into the way God wants you to mirror him and his bride. Awaken to the kind of beauty he's created for one man and one woman.

Don't go through all of the heartache the world says is normal. Blaze a different path. Sacrifice for each other, be vulnerable with each other, and desire transcendence together. Turn the way you do relationships on its head. Know that to get something that is above and beyond, you must do what is above and beyond.

> A new commandment I give to you, that you love one another: just as I have loved you, you also are to love one another. By this all people will know that you are my disciples, if you have love for one another (John 13:34-35).

Make the Choice, Change Your Life

I remember seeing her and feeling the air in my throat turn to cement. The necklace I'd given her, the necklace she said she'd always wear as a symbol of her love for me, was gone.

My world crashed.

Our relationship couldn't end this way. (We'd been separated for two months at this point with no hope in sight.) We couldn't just *make* God first in our lives. What did that even mean? Read my Bible more? Pray more?

I hid myself in my room, finding it nearly impossible to breathe. "You don't know what love is," I remember my dad saying. He left and I pressed my back against the wall, sliding into a crouch and feeling like God's first mistake.

If I was not truly in love, what was I feeling? Why did these moments feel like mountains?

For months after that talk, profound darkness ruled my life. Within the silence of my room, I'd press my fingernails into my arms, feel invisible strings pull my face taut, and weep.

I was falling at maximum speed. I was crashing.

I'd put something lesser in the place Jesus belonged. I wasn't capable of giving Brittney what she needed most because I refused to accept that I needed Christ more than her.

Thankfully, mercifully, Jesus changed that.

What's Next

When it comes to the *how* of relationships, there's no end of scenarios and situations. With that in mind, the next chapter is going to address some of the overarching questions that come with a decision to fly, such as: What should I look for in a potential other? How do I know if I'm ready? What if my other isn't interested in flying? How does online dating work with flying?

4

FLYING Q&A

You're not trying to replace God by finding your perfect
match—that's desperation. You are already perfectly
loved and looking for someone who can help you
grow in and share that love—that's security.

GARY THOMAS

How Do I Know If I'm Ready to Fly?

The best way to know whether or not you're ready is to honestly answer these three questions:

- Am I willing to do a hard thing for what might seem like a long time, as others say I am dumb or crazy for doing it?
- Do I possess what I need to give?
- Is my ultimate purpose for this relationship focused on the possibility of marriage?

If your answers to these questions are *yes*, and you mean them, you're ready to fly.

Sure, there are other issues that factor into whether or not you should be in a relationship right now—such as your emotional wholeness and general maturity—but these three questions are the biggies.

Are you willing to sacrifice what you want now over and over again? Are you truly connecting with Jesus, or just claiming the title of Christian? Also consider: *Am I gentle and patient? Do I serve? Am I loyal? Generous? Honest? Self-controlled?*

And concerning marriage: Do you really see your other as someone you might spend the rest of your life with, or are you just lying to yourself so you can have some good times with him or her? There's a poisonous deceit within all of us that we must be aware of (Jeremiah 17:9). Remember this while gauging whether or not you're ready to fly.

What Should I Look for in a Potential Other?

In his book *The Sacred Search*, Gary Thomas lists several practical things to look for in the other, such as:

> The Bible and all relationship research is very clear on this issue: people who can handle confrontation and feedback are the ones who can make relationships work.
>
> Henry Cloud and
> John Townsend[1]

Does the potential other fear God? Are they a true believer? How about a hard worker? Do they encourage people, or use words to hurt others? Do they exude peacefulness, or are they quarrelsome?

What Jesus-like attributes do they truly live out? What do they think about when they think about God? Does their theology inform how they live? How do they talk when speaking of Jesus? Do they speak well of others and respond well when confronted with sin? Or do they blame others, rationalize sin, and forget about God when trouble hits?

Look for someone who loves Jesus. Not just someone who goes to church or reads the Bible. Someone who is humble, who forgives, who resolves conflict well, and who knows how to communicate and be a good friend.

Seeking the opinion of those you love and trust is another wise thing to do when considering whether or not to move toward a relationship with someone. You don't want to get so picky that you're extending zero grace, of course.

> That's what you should be looking for: can this person walk with me toward God?
>
> Gary Thomas[2]

Simply try to gauge whether the other is someone you could see yourself pursuing Christ with.

How Does Online Dating Work with Flying?

Relationships that begin online are common. Does this work with flying? Yes. Because giving your other what's needed most over taking what's wanted now can be applied to any sort of interaction between you and your other.

But online relationships don't come without challenges and safety concerns. Similar to those who feel empowered to display obscene gestures while in a vehicle, people tend to say and do things online they'd never say or do in person. Plenty of predators lurk on websites and social media as well.

> Feelings of attraction and a desire for the opposite sex are powerful realities in our lives. If these are not anchored by your values about the Christian life (e.g. sexual purity, local church, fellowship) they will pull you towards either conflict or compromise.
>
> Isaac Hydoski[3]

That said, if you're getting to know another follower of Jesus online, Isaac Hydoski of Covenant Life Church suggests the following: 1) Discern your motives; 2) involve your community; 3) know your values and convictions; 4) communicate your values and convictions; and 5) ask about their values and convictions.

Other good things to remember include:

- Aim to build respect.
- Point to Jesus.
- Make purity a priority.
- Paint an entire picture of who you are instead of hiding the less attractive aspects of yourself.

How Do You Introduce Your Other to Flying?

Tell your other that there's something you want to talk about and then sit down together. You don't want to freak him or her out, but you want to make the talk weighty enough that both of you can talk seriously.

Start the conversation with Jesus and your desire to love as he loves. To give what's needed most over taking what's wanted now: physically, emotionally, and spiritually. Then move into the three pillars of flying.

Discuss why you'd like to practice more selflessness in the relationship. Talk about the kind of vulnerability you'd like to stir up between you and your other. Then get real about the fact that you believe loving like Jesus, though difficult, is a transcendent kind of love that will forever change your relationship.

At this point, your other will most likely nod and like what you're saying. The real test is when you get into what flying might change about your relationship, such as physical and emotional boundaries, the hard work of planning for success, and setting your sights on obeying Christ.

Like most things that go against the norm, these conversations aren't easy. They can be difficult and awkward. But they're necessary. They're worth it. Don't shy away from saying what needs to be said or doing what needs to be done.

What If My Other Wants to Fly but Hasn't Found Their Identity in Jesus?

If your other places their identity in you rather than in Jesus, you've got a problem. If you are to experience the transcendent kind of love God has designed, both of you must love Christ more than each other. I know that sounds kind of super spiritual, but it's just the plain truth.

Loving Jesus more than your other helps you love your other more than you ever thought possible. So if he or she hasn't found identity in Christ, the best thing you can do is help your other cling to Jesus more than to you.

Sometimes this means diving deep into discussions. Intentionally doing things in your relationship that point you both toward Jesus. And staying open and honest about your relationship with Christ.

But other times, it means separating from each other. This is what Dustin and Mary needed in their relationship.

Though both attended the same Christian college and had put their trust in Jesus, Dustin in particular struggled with finding his identity in Jesus. He clung to Mary and spiraled into doubt and depression when she couldn't hang out with him regularly. And when they were together, he wanted to get as physical as possible to feel connected to her. These are signs of someone who's feeding his or her soul with another human—not Christ.

Mary initiated a separation for a few months, Dustin got good counsel from some mature followers, and when they came back together, it was much sweeter. It hurts like crazy parting ways for a time, but sometimes that's exactly what you and your other need to truly get intimate with God.

What If My Other Isn't Interested in a Flying Relationship?

If you're in a falling relationship and want to start flying but your other doesn't, ask yourself these questions:

- Is my other's disinterest grounded in what God says or in what's easy?

- Is my other's desire to love me like Jesus? Or just in his or her own way?

- What do my answers to the first two questions say about my other?

> If the person you are interested in is not someone with whom you believe you can seek God's kingdom and pursue a life of righteousness, that's a deal breaker.
>
> Gary Thomas[4]

Fact is, you're not just looking for someone to agree to fly with you. You're looking for someone who will inspire you to be more like Jesus. Does that describe your other? If so, what's keeping him or her from wanting to give what's needed most?

WHEN WHAT'S NEEDED MOST IS A BREAKUP

Sometimes the best way to give your other what he or she needs most is to break up. That might be the last thing you ever wanted to hear, but hear me out.

If you don't see the relationship ever progressing toward marriage, you're stealing your other's time and emotion. If you know they're putting you above Jesus and are showing no signs of turning to him, you're contributing to their idolatry. If you know the timing isn't right or that there are just too many theological differences between you and your other, you're holding onto something that just isn't meant to be.

Separating from a special other is one of the most painful things the human heart can experience. But at the end of the day, in scenarios such as these, it's right and good for both of you.

What If My Other Doesn't Know Jesus?

The entire purpose of a relationship is to discover whether or not you and your other are fit to marry. But God doesn't want us marrying unless it's to someone who shines with the light of Jesus (2 Corinthians 6:14). Reason tells us, then, that if someone doesn't know Jesus, the relationship shouldn't ever begin.

I know that isn't easy to hear.

Perhaps you recently became a Christian but your other is not. Perhaps you're dating a nonbeliever in hopes of introducing him or her to Jesus. And all you want is for another Christian to listen to you instead of telling you to break up.

This is a tough one, friend. Because there isn't an answer that isn't going to hurt. I could say, "Go and fly regardless of your nonbelieving other," and bring you temporary relief. Or I could say "Breaking up is the thing to do," and bring you temporary pain.

But the truth is that the temporary relief will yield long-term pain, and the temporary pain will yield long-term relief.

It's not that I know the future. It's that I've looked at enough pasts to know this is true. Are there exceptions? Of course. But dating someone who doesn't know and love God is asking for a tremendous amount of heartache. If not now, then when you're married. And if not in your early marriage, then when you have children.

Going into a relationship looking to change someone is to set yourself up for extreme difficulty and pain. Relationships are not the place for evangelism, nor are marriages the place for character reform.

So if your other doesn't know Jesus, the very best thing you can do is break it off, surround yourself with brothers and sisters who will love you through your grief and mourning, and cling to Christ.

Do not be yoked together with unbelievers. For what do righteousness and wickedness have in common? Or what fellowship can light have with darkness? What harmony is there between Christ and Belial, or what does a believer have in common with an unbeliever? (2 Corinthians 6:14-15).

Mark Driscoll offers three reasons why we shouldn't date unbelievers: First, a nonbeliever can't even begin to understand who you are since they don't know Jesus. Second, since Scripture is the highest authority in a Christian marriage, a relationship with someone who doesn't trust the Bible leaves you in a position to have two value systems that often contradict each other. Third, when tough times come, and they will, you will have no means of dealing with sin that comes between the two of you.[5]

What's the Most Important Thing I Can Do Before My Next Relationship?

Pursue a deeper satisfaction in your relationship with Jesus. Doing so not only prepares you to fly, but also prevents you from falling with someone.

If your soul is anything less than satisfied in the abundant life Jesus offers, if you find yourself lost in loneliness or lack fulfillment, then you'll ultimately look to your other to bridge the gap—the exact opposite of what flying is all about.

I know it's incredibly hard being alone. I know the chasm it creates in the heart and I feel your hurt. I'm not here to say you're somehow wrong in your aloneness—that would be straight-up heresy. I'm simply here to say that Jesus is the only remedy for it.

Pursuing a deeper satisfaction in Christ isn't the kind of answer that's going to go viral. But it's the absolute best thing you can do before your next relationship.

Come to me, all who labor and are heavy laden, and I will give you rest. Take my yoke upon you, and learn from me, for I am gentle and lowly in heart, and you will find rest

for your souls. For my yoke is easy, and my burden is light
(Matthew 11:28-30).

What's Next

Flying requires that you give your other what's needed most. But
how do you know if you have what your other needs? This is what we
will explore in the next chapter.

Part 2

WHAT YOUR OTHER NEEDS MOST

5

WHERE TO START

You cannot love a fellow creature fully till you love God.

C.S. LEWIS

A drugged-up mother having a heart-to-heart with her daughter about making right choices. An adulterous father telling his son that he shouldn't look at pornography. One word encapsulates this kind of advice: hypocrisy.

We cannot give what we do not have.

Early in my relationship with Brittney, I didn't have what it took to fly. I desperately wanted to give her the utmost love any human could give another. But because I didn't know what that meant or looked like, I ended up doing the exact opposite—taking what I wanted instead of giving what both of us needed most.

That's the way relationships work. If you don't know how to fly, you'll ultimately fall.

What You Must Gain Before You Can Give

Ever played a video game in which you can't advance because you're missing something? Growing up, this sort of thing drove me nuts. Getting stuck midway through a conquest made me want to call the game-makers and say, *I've done everything I can think to do. But I can't get any further without someone telling me how. Do you even* want *me to finish?*

> For it is not mere words that nourish the soul, but God Himself, and unless and until the hearers find God in personal experience they are not the better for having heard the truth.
>
> A.W. Tozer[1]

This is what I felt like when I finally decided to stop falling with Brittney and start flying instead. I knew exactly what I needed to do—stop idolizing her and start learning to love like Jesus—but I had no idea how to proceed. I felt like raising my hands to heaven and saying, *Here I am—but what's next?*

This is the place we all must reach if we're to gain what we want to give. The place we discover that in order to give our other the greatest love, we must first intimately know and pursue the Greatest Lover.

Jesus Christ.

It seems like an oxymoron, but in order to love your other to your ultimate capacity, you must love Jesus more than him or her. If you do not sow a deep relationship with Christ, who is the essence of love, you cannot impart anything but a lesser love to your other. Your romance will only ever be as amazing as your intimacy with Christ. To have a so-so relationship with him is to offer your other a so-so relationship.

But listen: I know how ho-hum this Jesus-first talk can sound, especially if you've grown up Christian. *Yeah, it's all about Jesus. What's new? How do I actually turn this into a lifestyle?*

Closeness > Complacency

It's been said that if you want to know whether or not someone is alive, don't look for the person's birth certificate—check for a pulse.

Many believers claim to have a personal relationship with Christ. But what exactly does that mean? Is it a decision, or a drive? A fact, or a fruit? A certificate, or a pulse? I'm not implying that you must work for your relationship with Jesus. I'm implying that a relationship in which you're inactive isn't a relationship at all.

There may not be a more dangerous, soul-eating virus than that of complacency in your relationship with Jesus.

I think that's why Scripture tells us to work out our salvation with fear and trembling (Philippians 2:12). To be strong and immovable, always working enthusiastically for Christ (1 Corinthians 15:58). To crave for a deeper relationship with Jesus through the understanding of him (1 Peter 2:1-3). To love him with an intense, committed love that we give to no one else (Luke 14:26). And to live as though our time to live for him were coming to an end (1 Peter 4:7).

"Personal relationship with Christ" doesn't mean much if we're presuming upon it. That's just impersonal. For it to be personal requires pursuit, commitment, intimacy.

Are you close with Jesus? Do you talk to him as if he's your best friend, or is he a stranger to you? Do you look for him in everyday life, or do you just go about your day?

Closeness with Jesus changes everything in your life and the way you do relationships. It frees you from fears and insecurities. It makes you at peace with your circumstances. It helps you choose what your other needs most over what you want now. These are not things you can work on in a relationship. These come through closeness with Jesus alone.

Herein lies our great problem. How do you pursue a relationship with someone you cannot see with your eyes, hear with your ears, or touch with your hands? How do you thirst for God as a deer pants for flowing streams? Experience his calming, joyful, everlasting love? Earnestly seek him and gaze upon his power and glory in soul-satisfying surrender?

Sometimes I wish it were as simple as a decision, a flick of a switch. But a relationship takes work. And a relationship with a person you cannot see takes extra work.

But this work is not in vain.

As we draw near to God, he promises to draw near to us. As we acknowledge him in everything we do, he makes our way clear. As we seek first the kingdom of God and his righteousness, everything else is added unto us.

When these things happen, your life is never the same in the most beautiful way.

> Let us then with confidence draw near to the throne of grace, that we may receive mercy and find grace to help in time of need (Hebrews 4:16).

Anatomy of a Relationship

Brittney and I start nearly every day with a coffee date. It's how we connect with each other before distractions hit. We talk about anything, everything, and nothing. Sometimes we just sit and watch the fire burn. Other times we goof off and make each other spit java all over the carpet.

But when we go a day or two without a coffee date, both of us notice a change in our chemistry. We can't focus on our work. We get irritable, feel out of sync, and just seem distant.

The relationship you and I share with Jesus, though spiritual, isn't different.

If we don't communicate with God and spend quality time with him, something in our soul feels off, rendering us useless to go about our lives loving like he loves.

This is why we all must consider how we're actively pursuing closeness with God. Again, not to earn our relationship with him. But to simply have a relationship with him.

Without communication and quality time with God, we simply cannot fly.

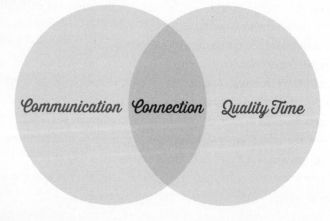

Communication

If you've given your life to Christ, he's sent the Holy Spirit to dwell inside you, comfort you, and prompt you to action. He's given you a direct connection to his will. Empowered you to live differently, love differently, and speak differently.

This includes how you act toward your other.

The Spirit gives you the patience you lack, the kindness and encouraging words you need, and the truthfulness that's so vital in your relationship with your other. He helps you put on the clothing of real humility, not the false humility we so

> We are made to long for God, to be restless until we rest in God. When we expect to find satisfaction of our desires in another person, we fool ourselves.
>
> Laura Smit[2]

often dress ourselves in when we're trying to impress. He pours out of you when opportunities arise to glorify Jesus. He gives you eyes to see your other as a brother or sister—not a sex object or anything else that leaves you wanting to take instead of give. He actively searches you for any mixed motives in your relationship. He convicts you and draws you to your knees.

The more in tune you are with the Spirit, the more he moves you to do what magnifies Jesus.

But do you live connected to the Spirit—or disconnected? Do you presume upon the role of the Spirit—or do you engage in that role? It makes a difference in your life. A big difference.

Without reliance on the Spirit, it's impossible to feel true comfort, understand truth, feel convicted of sin, or discern when and how to take action. It's impossible to live a life of joy, peace, patience, kindness, goodness, faithfulness, or gentleness (Galatians 5:22-23).

When you are attentively aware of God's Spirit, you understand his will for you in hour-to-hour living—even when it doesn't seem to make sense. You live with a calming, courageous power beyond your comprehension.

Ask God right now for a more intimate connection with his Spirit. Ask him to put an end to whatever ignorance you have toward him. Literally pray, *Lord God, stir up your Spirit inside me. Calm me as you've promised. I stand ready for whatever you have for me.*

Go through your day asking, *How do you want to use me? What part can I play in your glory?* To live in the Spirit is to shout "Here am I; send me!" (Isaiah 6:8) every moment of every day. It's like raising your hand at all times so that when the time comes and God is looking to show himself strongly through his children, he looks at you and says, "That's the one I'm going to use."

> If you then, who are evil, know how to give good gifts to
> your children, how much more will the heavenly Father
> give the Holy Spirit to those who ask him! (Luke 11:13).

Quality Time

God gave us Scripture to reveal truth, teach us to love, and show us how to live rightly. He gave us prayer to fellowship with him as children do with their father.

To open the Bible or drop to our knees is to enfold our hearts with his purpose for our lives. But is that what you experience when you read Scripture or pray?

Truth is, most of us neuter the power of these direct links to God. We approach them as duties rather than privileges, super spiritual things we do only when we're *feeling* super spiritual. We think of them flippantly as though Scripture and prayer contain no power or mystery. We look to get what we want instead of looking for what God has for us.

God didn't give us the Bible or command that we pray to burden us. He didn't give them to us as stagnant practices that do not change our lives. He gave them so we could participate in his grand plan of redemption.

He gave them to help us love like Jesus.

This is why we must intentionally create quality ways to read the Bible and pray.

If I had coffee with Brittney every day but stared at my phone the whole time, or sat down with her reluctantly, or simply spoke the whole time but never listened, there'd be no relationship. Time would be spent, but none of it would be valuable. None of it would be quality.

What makes time with Brittney quality is when I'm being real with her. Respecting her. Adoring her. We must aspire to the same in how we read Scripture and pray.

Come messy: Don't let sin stop you from approaching God in prayer or reading his Word. God isn't a God of perfect people. He's the God of sinners whom he dearly loves and gave his Son for. To believe we must clean ourselves up to approach him is a mockery of his grace. He wants us to come as we are, warts and all.

Come reverent: Coming to God messy doesn't mean we should come to him as slobs. God is the Alpha and the Omega, the beginning and the end—and we should always have a proper fear of his transcendent self. Just like we wouldn't walk into the White House as if we owned the place, we shouldn't approach God as though he somehow deserves less reverence than we give to important people on earth. So come humble. Come repentant of your sin and eager for Christ's righteousness.

Come as a child: God is our Father. He is the one who came running to greet us, wrapped a robe around us, and threw a party in our name (Luke 15:11-32). God is the most personal being in the universe. He doesn't want us cowering as we approach him. He wants us delighting in him. He wants us to anticipate being with him forever in heaven.

Connection

When Brittney and I communicate and spend quality time together, we become connected. United. Locked in. No tension remains. We are prepared for whatever life throws our way because no matter how disconnected we may become outwardly, we are always connected inwardly.

So it is in our relationship with God.

Intimacy with the Holy Spirit and quality time in prayer and God's Word equip you to not only respond to life, but to redeem it. You become so in tune with your God-given purpose that no matter how hard life gets, you react as Jesus would.

Instead of selfishness, you choose selflessness. Instead of fearing criticism, you choose vulnerability. Instead of being like everyone else, you choose the transcendent way of Christ. No longer are you just someone who goes to church. You are a follower whose very soul is going through amazing changes that make you a giver instead of a taker, a lover instead of a hater, a strong presence even in your weakness.

This is what you and I were created for.

It's time you break free and truly worship and connect with your King. To finally cling to him with everything you are. To become more intimate with him than you are with any other human being. To gain not only what your other desperately needs you to give—but what you desperately need for yourself.

> The highest love of God is not intellectual, it is spiritual. God is spirit and only the spirit of man can know Him really. In the deep spirit of man the fire must glow or his love is not the true love of God.
>
> A.W. Tozer[3]

Closeness with Jesus.

A word of caution, though. If your primary purpose for giving your life to God is so that you can do relationships better, then you've missed the point. God isn't a means to an end. He is the end. The reason this chapter exists isn't so you can tweak your relationship with God to get a better result in your relationship. It's to help you dive deeper into your relationship with God and, ultimately, become more like Jesus in how you do all of life.

It's not easy to give yourself over to the Holy Spirit. It's not easy to pursue God in prayer or immerse yourself in his Word. But when you invest in your relationship with your Creator, he will fashion a new and beautiful desire inside you.

A desire to live and love like his Son.

I don't remember the exact day I finally desired Christ more than Brittney. But when it came, I remember thinking that my heavenly relationship with God would never hinder my earthly relationship with Brittney. It would only ever enable it and make it more beautiful.

Closeness with Jesus gives you the ability to love like you've never loved. It

> You stir man to take pleasure in praising you, because you have made us for yourself, and our heart is restless until it rests in you.
>
> St. Augustine[4]

opens your eyes to see what's needed most instead of blindly taking what's wanted now. It's never easy, but it's always better. It's never natural, but it's always beautiful. This is the essence of flying.

You ready?

What's Next

When we intentionally pursue a relationship with Jesus and fully give our lives to him, he intentionally teaches us John 15:12 love. He performs surgery on our heart as we slowly begin to love others as he loves us. What this looks like is what the next few chapters explore.

Ask Those Who Fly

Did you ever make an idol of your other? How?

It is shockingly easy to make an idol of our relationship. Every day, we have the choice to spend our time focusing on our relationship or focusing on Christ. And if we are truly honest, more often than not, we are focusing on our relationship, or on each other, far more. It's hard to remember that focusing on Christ and keeping our relationship strong with him actually benefits our relationship as a whole.

Jake & Sarah

I think both of us might have been guilty of falling into this trap from time to time. It was the first serious relationship for Isaac, and my absolute first relationship, so it was difficult to not become overwhelmed by the sheer wonder of it all. However, in those times, Isaac in particular was good about having both of us pray together and steer the focus back to the Lord.

Melissa

How difficult was it to love Jesus more than your other?

We were so excited about getting to know each other that our relationship often trumped everything else in our lives, including Christ. We found it way too easy to be satisfied in our blossoming love for one another instead of in our Savior. We worked hard at this issue and pursued Jesus intentionally, but it certainly didn't come naturally or easily.

Andrew & Abigail

Calibrating my thinking with the eternal reality that Kristi is my mate only for this life has helped us keep the right perspective on our relationship. Our relationship is not an end in itself; it is simply a temporary reflection of Christ and his bride, the church. As such, we get to enjoy Christ and each other in a much deeper context than we otherwise could. Our relationship, though temporary, points to the *ultimate* love story in eternity: Jesus wooing and winning his bride.

Josh

What advice would you give to someone who's struggled with making an idol of their other?

Really seeking Jesus through consistent prayer and Bible reading is what we recommend for combatting the idol problem. Renewing your mind with truth about God's sufficiency is a great way to stay reminded of where you can find real joy. A boyfriend, girlfriend, or spouse is going to disappoint if that's where you're looking for satisfaction, but Jesus and what he did for you will never change.

Andrew & Abigail

You will always be disappointed if you look for your value anywhere but in your relationship with Christ. If it is on this earth, it will disappoint you. It will break, it will hurt us, and ultimately, it will not last. Even the relationships we work so hard to cultivate. It is our daily goal to point one another to Christ, to our need for a savior, and not to each other. This is the only way to true peace and joy, and it is the only way to truly love our significant other.

Jake & Sarah

Stay in Scripture and solid Christian teaching. Reckon the truths of the Bible to be true of *your* life. Strive to flush pop-culture and self-help ideas about relationships out of your thinking. Take every thought captive and consciously reject the thoughts that don't line up with Truth.

Josh

Read the Gospels. Is your other really cooler than Jesus? More than that, I'd challenge them to identify what the gospel truly is. If they can do that—I mean really articulate it and see how it affects every facet of life—then "other idolatry" should become a non-issue. Your other is a sinner who needs the gospel too!

Matt

Look at your relationship as a triangle, with God as the top point and each other as the bottom two points. If you keep your eyes on God and keep moving toward him, you find that you come closer together as a couple. But if you take your eyes off God and start moving in the other direction, you end up further apart than ever.

Jen & Tyler

6

WHO YOU MUST WATCH OUT FOR

Purity is not about not having sex.
It's about waiting to have it right.

Dannah Gresh

Imagine your best friend is about to date someone you know is a good person, but who's acted suspiciously in the past. What might scare you about their budding relationship? To what lengths would you go to lovingly support but protect your friend? Think about that for a moment. What would you do? What would you say?

Here's the thing: You are the suspicious person, and the friend in the story is your special other.

Even if you are like a signpost always pointing to Jesus, you are still the greatest threat to your relationship. That's the mindset you must have if you want to give your other what he or she needs most. I'm not talking about hating or abusing yourself. I'm talking about acknowledging that even your best intentions will fail when they're competing with the desires of your heart.

Desires like wanting to get more physical than is appropriate.

Or talking in ways you shouldn't.

Or letting thoughts and feelings for your other displace your thoughts and feelings for Jesus.

Don't get me wrong. There's nothing wrong with growing madly in love. That's the direction relationships should move. But this kind of crazy love needs to overflow out of your ultimate love and obedience to God.

To consider yourself your own worst enemy prepares you to win the fights no one but you know exist. And it gets humbling really fast, because it requires an almost uncomfortable level of self-awareness. But getting humbled by your capacity for sin is a good thing. Because many of us think we can handle ourselves. I know that's what I thought.

And I was wrong.

There's a reason why God asks us if a person can carry fire and not get burned (Proverbs 6:27-28). A reason why he doesn't merely tell us to be mindful of sexual immorality, but to run from it (1 Corinthians 6:18). A reason why he says we must put impurity to death (Colossians 3:5). A reason why he says the one who does what his flesh wants him to do will reap corruption (Galatians 6:8). A reason why he says our fleshly passions wage war against our souls (1 Peter 2:11). A reason why he instructs us to leave no room for the flesh to do what it wants (Romans 13:14). A reason why he says the heart is deceitful above all things—and desperately sick (Jeremiah 17:9).

> Romantic feelings can be very deceptive, and even pathological.
>
> Henry Cloud and John Townsend[1]

We need to be aware of our sinful desires and act upon that awareness. Strategize for success. Look for ways to give our other what's needed most in moments when our hearts and bodies want something now.

In guarding against sins of the body, you:

> Temptations are not sins. What we do with those temptations is the issue.
>
> Shaunti Feldhahn[2]

- protect the source from which flows everything else in your life (Proverbs 4:23)
- stay physically unblemished for your other (Hebrews 13:4)
- actively worship God (Romans 12:1)
- and escape the unique soul-eating sin of sinning against your own body (1 Corinthians 6:18).

That's what this chapter is about.

The prudent sees danger and hides himself (Proverbs 27:12).

Save Your Other from Yourself

One of the saddest realities about falling relationships is that many believe dabbling in regretful scenarios is a part of the process. Things like getting in bed with each other, doing everything but the act of sex, indulging in intense make-out sessions, making premature vows to each other, or getting so addicted with each other that both lose touch with reality.

> If someone cannot delay gratification and control himself or herself in this area, what makes you think that they can delay their own gratification in other areas of sacrifice for you? What is going to curb the "I want what I want now" mentality in the rest of life?
>
> Henry Cloud
> and John Townsend[3]

When Brittney and I started dating after a very long separation, I thought keeping God first in our relationship would be easy. I mean, we had both spent two and a half years growing deeper in our affection and commitment to him, loving and studying his Word, and just going about life in reliance on him. How could we fall into something less than a beautiful, God-honoring relationship?

In many ways I learned.

A sweet moment in conversation can quickly become touching each other in ways you shouldn't. Your time spent getting to know Jesus more deeply can quickly become time daydreaming about your other and completely forgetting about God. Desperate pleading for God's help one night can quickly become a foolish sprint into the same sin the next morning.

Looking back, I'm still a bit baffled at how quickly my firm convictions and resolve to do the right thing crumbled. I entered our relationship with a strong desire to please God. How did I ever slip up?

It's simple: Intentions and convictions cannot survive without discipline—the discipline to talk with God fervently, plan wisely, and react immediately. Without it, the firm boundaries you settle upon in your own heart will melt into goo.

If you are determined to pursue physical and emotional purity, a pledge with yourself isn't going to last. If you want God to be the heartbeat of your relationship, it won't happen just because it's what you desire most. You need to be very intentional in saving both you and your other from yourself.

In 1 Timothy 5:2, Paul tells Timothy to treat younger women in all purity as sisters. To physically treat each other as a brother or sister is a good starting point for a pure relationship. Obviously, it's more complicated than that, as there are physical things couples do that brothers and sisters don't. But one simple fact remains: Brothers and sisters do not make sexual advances.

If you and your other have repented of sin and given your lives to Jesus, then you are children of God. And like the good father he is, he wants the best for his kids. Including your purity and holiness. You need to take this seriously. Pinpoint areas of danger in your relationship and eliminate them. When you or your other push against physical boundaries, you are going against the perfect way of your Father.

> Watch and pray that you may not enter into temptation. The spirit indeed is willing, but the flesh is weak (Matthew 26:41).

The Infamous Slippery Slope Analogy

During my separation from Brittney, I'd periodically meet with her dad. One story he told me was that of the slippery slope.

When you sled down a hill of fresh snow, you don't go very fast. The snow isn't packed yet. It's fluffy. But the more times you sled down, the slicker it becomes. And by the end of the day, you're shooting down the hill like a torpedo.

> We were created to be addicted—glued—to the person we have sex with. But just to one. And not until we're committed by a marriage covenant. Or our hearts get hurt.
>
> Dannah Gresh[4]

Brittney and I had grown so emotionally attached that it wouldn't take much to push us all the way. In other words, if we kept growing closer it would be very difficult to avoid sex before marriage.

And even though I didn't agree with him at the time, he was right.

What is your emotional and physical status with your other right now? If you're just beginning your relationship, you're in a great place to discuss how you can give each other what's needed most in the realm of physical boundaries. If you already have regrets, it's vital to commit yourself to purity right now so you can stop taking what isn't yours. Not just because you want to be a good Christian. But because you want to honor God's commands. Don't let the issue linger another day. It will only get worse.

> Can a man carry fire next to his chest and his clothes not be burned? Or can one walk on hot coals and his feet not be scorched? (Proverbs 6:27-28).

Boundaries Don't Work

If you want to honor God in your relationship, you need something far more powerful than boundaries. The fact is, boundaries are like those pleasant exchanges you have when you run into someone you haven't seen in a while and say something like, *We should get together sometime*. You might like the idea, but you probably won't put much effort into making it happen.

> Someone who is trying to please God shouldn't be asking how close to the edge he or she can go before crossing the line.
>
> Rebecca St. James[5]

Boundaries are merely good intentions that deceivingly promise success. Like dieting pills or get-rich-quick schemes. We set boundaries such as no kissing, no sex, or no physical contact whatsoever. But as we grow more comfortable and more attracted to one another, we push against the fences thinking we're okay so long as we don't cross.

Then we cross.

In a split second, the deceit of your heart renders your boundaries useless. In a split second, everything you've wanted to shelter is exposed. What's worse, you most likely won't react in horror. You'll instead think,

Wow—never been beyond the fence before. That's just how we operate: wanting what is forbidden. Conviction doesn't hit first when boundaries are crossed. Euphoria does.

And that euphoria can lead to sexual sin—whether or not you actually have sex. We don't need boundaries. We need uncrossable moats.

> Over the course of a five-year study, researchers learned that 42 percent of 15- to 17-year-olds, 72 percent of 18- to 19-year-olds, and 84 percent of 20- to 24-year-olds have participated in sexual activity.[6]

Moats Work

Here are two examples of moats, and they're not fun.

1. We commit to always being in a place where others can see us.

2. We each ask a mentor to keep us true to number 1.

> Sex is a means to celebrate commitment, and that's why it is so destructive outside of commitment. With each new partner comes a new bond that either *follows* you or *desensitizes* you.
>
> Tyler McKenzie[7]

Moats are difficult, impractical, and get a lot of criticism—even from people who love you. Brittney and I had the moat of no driving in the same car together, and we hated it. But the truth is, it helped save us from ourselves. If you have a no-alone policy, you won't get physical with each other. And if you have consistent talks with a mentor, you have to own up to whether or not you're staying true to your no-alone policy. These moats help you avoid becoming a statistic.

People will tell you that moats stunt growth in your relationship. And if you interpret not being alone together as never having a private conversation together, they have a point. So always remember this rule about moats: Only build a moat after you've discussed how to solve the potential problems that come with it.

By driving separate cars, the only dilemma Brittney and I faced was gas money. As inconvenient as this moat was, it didn't stunt our relationship.

If you make the choice to never be alone, you first need to work out how you'll be able to have private conversations and leisure time together. This may mean doing most of your dating at coffee shops, parks, or some other public place.

I know this isn't a popular idea.

Seriously, who wants to take precaution against the possibility of failure when everything seems perfectly okay? We'd rather grit our teeth and muscle through the temptation. But the reality is that this kind of inconvenience makes flying relationships possible.

Moats are not fun. They're not natural. But taking what's not yours and disobeying God is much worse. The statistics are desperate. And desperate times call for drastic measures.

Moats are a drastic measure—but they're worth it. Have you considered what it might feel like to ask your future other...*How many girls have you touched?* Or *How many guys have you made out with?* That's painful stuff. These are irreversible exchanges between two people—exchanges of a deep physical sacredness God intends us to protect until marriage. One of the benefits of moats is that, if the relationship doesn't work out, you and your other can end it in a way that, yes, still hurts, but saves a deep part of yourself that God designed for marriage.

> So flee youthful passions and pursue righteousness, faith, love, and peace, along with those who call on the Lord from a pure heart (2 Timothy 2:22).

Get Vocal with Each Other

Actually taking the time to discuss how you want to obey God with your bodies—and how you're going to do it—is difficult. But this is how you set yourself up for success.

Consider saying something like this:

I really like you and want what's best for both of us no matter what. Here's the thing: I really want to honor Jesus in every part of our relationship and keep him first. But I know that even the best people betray their good intensions—like David. So here's what I'm thinking...

From there, it's up to you to get vulnerable about whatever moats you'd like to dig, whether they be physical, emotional, or spiritual.

You have to be extremely brave in relationships. One of you has to take the first step vocally.

Be the first. This is where respect is built and where trust is made. Look your other in the eyes and address the elephant in the room: physical boundaries. These are hard conversations. Nobody wants to talk about the possibility of failure. But these talks can do a world of good if you keep the focus on honoring God.

Watch What You Say and How You Say It

I'm a romantic at heart. I like writing Brittney poems, twirling her around the dance floor, and holding her hand whenever I can. But being a romantic got me in trouble at times in my relationship with Brittney—especially in how I spoke. The tongue is very powerful. It has the power to stir up so much emotion in another human being. With it you can do great good and great evil. The worst part? The tongue is also tricky. Or, to be more precise, we are tricky—our motives.

I played with fire in this area with Brittney. I knew she loved me— she'd filled dozens of journals about me!—but I always yearned to hear it again: that she loved me, loved me, loved me.

Part of this yearning was tied to my own insecurity, for sure. But somewhere deep in my heart, it seems I also wanted her to love me more than she loved God. (Not that I ever thought that. It's just how I see my behavior in retrospect.) Instead of using my words to lift her eyes to God, I used them to lower her eyes to me. By doing so, I was shoving God out of Brittney's life and shoving myself into the center of it.

Don't get me wrong. There's nothing bad about falling head over heels in love. The problem occurs when infatuation foils your relationship with God—which is easy to do if you're always using your tongue for your own satisfaction instead of for God's glory.

Look for ways to help your other radiate with love for Jesus, not you. And if that makes them fixate on you, awesome. If someone is going to love you, you want them loving the Jesus in you.

Brandon Andersen, executive pastor at Mars Hill Church Everett, offered the following suggestions as indicators that you may be crossing the line emotionally:[8]

- You just started dating, and you are sharing "heart" things with each other that you haven't shared with closest friends and/or mentors that you have known for years.

- You are isolating yourselves as a couple and not listening to people whose opinion you used to value (Prov. 15:22), saying things like, "They just don't understand what we have."

- Your individual Christian walks become intertwined, and you end up pursuing and becoming closer with each other over becoming closer with God.

Modesty Matters

Rules are not the centerpiece of modesty. Necklines and skirt lengths for girls and shirts on or off for guys isn't the big deal. The main issue of modesty is exactly what we've been talking about all along: giving what your other needs most instead of taking what you want now.

What does your other need most?

Safety from lust: As much as you want your other to find your body attractive, the dating relationship is supposed to be a testing time for true love and compatibility, not a tease of how sexy you are. Most men and women today struggle with lust. Get honest with yourself about what you wear or don't wear.

Safety from touching: When two people in love touch each other, sparks fly. It's a natural sensation. But if something feels good, you usually want more, more, more. Holding hands for the first time is electrifying, but not as electrifying after a week or two. So you try a kiss on the cheek, which leads to passionate kissing, and then something even more sensual. Doing this is like putting a steak on a Doberman's snout: You're going to get bit. As much as you want to, don't succumb to flirtatious touching. It won't end well.

Safety from your lips: Again, the tongue is powerful. The words you say or whisper to your other can make his or her head spin a hundred miles per hour. This can be a very bad thing if what you're saying is laced with sexuality. When you turn your other on, you're turning them off to God. And that's the worst thing you can do in the relationship. That's taking what you want, not giving what's needed most.

Don't Roll the Dice

Playing the dice game Farkle with Brittney's family, my seven-year-old brother-in-law was rolling like I'd never seen. Not only had he set a new record of points made in one turn, but he kept defying the odds by rolling for even more points—again and again. The look on his face cracked us up. He was loving every minute of it.

We warned him: "Timmy, if you don't roll a one or a five, all the points you've got so far will just go away."

He rolled again and got more points. So we urged again. "Timmy, your odds are not good if you roll again."

But without a thought, the dice shot out of his hand. No one. No five. Bust. And he burst into tears.

We all laugh about that story to this day.

In relationships, some of us like testing the odds. We put ourselves in potentially damaging situations because we want to know whether or not we can handle them. But just like rolling the dice over and over, there's a high probability for failure. If you test the odds once and succeed, you'll want to test them again. But this time you'll want to test them in a more dangerous context. And if you manage to pass that test, you'll try for something even harder.

What's worse is that as you continue beating the odds, you'll gain confidence. A voice will tell you that you've aced the test once and can ace it again. It will tell you that you've built up a sort of immunity to failure. But probability promises that you'll eventually roll a dice void of ones or fives.

Stepping a little closer to a cliff will never magically extend the ground beneath your feet. If you step, you fall. It's inevitable. Resist the urge to test the odds. Your other needs absolute safety, not a flippant roll of the dice.

Unless you have someone mentoring you already, it's up to you to recognize areas of danger in your relationship. Don't go somewhere if you predict temptation. Don't stay somewhere if your conscience is on red alert. Run. Get away from the danger.

> For this is the will of God, your sanctification: that you abstain from sexual immorality; that each one of you know how to control his own body in holiness and honor, not in the passion of lust like the Gentiles who do not know God (1 Thessalonians 4:3-5).

Cues You're in Danger

My wife and I work as night managers at some retirement apartments. When a resident is in trouble they can pull an emergency pull cord, which triggers an alarm in our apartment. A very loud alarm.

The alarm is so loud that it's not only impossible to sleep through—it's impossible to bear. The moment it goes off, I sprint to the control panel and silence it. Only then can I think clearly enough to assess the situation and take appropriate action.

Here's the thing: You have alarms that ring every time you and your other are in danger of hurting one another physically or emotionally. The problem is, you might not recognize them as alarms until the damage has been done.

Alarm 1: Your mind reels with the possibilities of failure. This alarm usually blares when the plans you have for the day or evening are different from anything you've ever done together—when you must bend your better judgment to fit the occasion. Beware, friend. If your mind starts reeling with all the possibilities of failure, recognize the alarm. Take action. Gather all of the precautionary weapons you have. If you don't, the alarm will begin sounding less and less like an alarm and more and more like a song. You slowly fade from cautiously fearful of falling into a trap to excitedly anticipating an opportunity of failure to arise. For most, that is a point of no return and sin is inevitable.

Alarm 2: Justifying. If you find yourself at a crossroads, uncertain whether or not a certain activity seems safe (like going to a movie together), listen carefully for this alarm. It's one thing to wisely consider all the reasons why the activity will be safe. It's another thing to justify doing it because other couples do it or because someone said it's no big deal. Basing your choices on other relationships is a very quick way to fall instead of fly. Whenever you start justifying, train your mind to hear it like an alarm.

Alarm 3: Compromising. Whenever you're in a position that compromises your convictions to keep your body pure and holy for marriage, you'll hear this alarm. Maybe you and your other are hanging out with another couple who want to watch a movie. And the next thing you know, the room is dark and blankets get passed around. Perhaps you've set a boundary that you won't ever be alone together, so you're good, right? *No*, this alarm says. Because the couple you're with doesn't care if you touch and kiss under the blanket. But, then again, you don't want to be awkward and say you can't watch the movie, right? This is how convictions get compromised. Don't let it happen in your relationship.

Alarm 4: Your heart starts racing. As noted before, if ignored, Alarm 1 will start sounding like a song. Your heart will race. Your body will tense. And nervous energy will course through you. It feels horrible and wonderful all at the same time because, even though you're excited, God's spirit is shouting, *Don't buy the lie. Run.* But it's hard to hear the Spirit clearly because the drug has kicked in—numbing you to the fact that you're about to disobey God and severely hurt your other. Mark this: When your heart races, pay attention. You may be in serious physical and emotional peril with your other.

> Each person is tempted when he is lured and enticed by his own desire. Then desire when it has conceived gives birth to sin, and sin when it is fully grown brings forth death (James 1:14-15).

Invite Others into Your Relationship

It's been said that wolves attack the lone sheep. And while it isn't pleasant to think of yourself or your other as a wolf, the reality is, we're all capable.

This is why it's vital to invite others into your relationship.

You'd think that if one of you were a wolf, preying on the other, that the victim would end the relationship. But that's not always the case. When you really like someone, it's like a drug. It numbs you to any pain you're feeling. Your heart is slowly being mutilated but you don't even feel it.

The people you bring into the relationship who love you and want to see you honor God won't let this happen. They see the claw marks, the blood, the bruises. And they'll help you—if you let them. Sometimes that's the hardest part. Because you want the relationship to work. You want to keep taking the drug until the wolf stops attacking and everything gets better.

But this only ends in disaster.

You need to ask the people you invite into your relationship to help you even when you'd rather take the drug. You need to recruit an honest team of people who truly care about the outcome of your relationship.

> If your friends and family say, "You're not the person you were before you became involved with _____," you need to find out what they mean.
>
> H. Norman Wright[9]

Recruit a support team. Tell them your desire to (1) mirror Jesus in your relationship, (2) save your other—and ultimately yourself—from yourself; and (3) do what it takes to keep yourself pure. Tell them that you want to talk, text, or email on a set schedule so the two of you can openly talk about the good, the bad, and the ugly of the relationship.

Give these loved ones permission to speak with you vulnerably about anything and everything they're observing in you and in the relationship. Be humble. Make it easy for them to help you. Because if the moment arises where they need to confront you, a part of you will resist. I encourage you to say something like, *Listen, I know I'm going to be tempted to lie to you when I screw up. I don't want to do that. So please, ask me all the hard questions—even ask me straight up if I've lied to you in any way. Twice if you have to.*

You need to be vulnerable to bring others into your relationship. In doing so, you're saying, *I know how capable I am of sinning against my other—would you please help me avoid that?* These aren't words you'd say to just anyone. You need to find someone who is wise, discerning, keeps secrets, and doesn't freak out or come unglued by brutal honesty. And, most importantly, someone whose only agenda is to honor God.

One of the reasons couples become dangers to each other is because they like each other so much that they'd rather be exclusive. Obviously it's important to reserve time for lots of private conversations as you get to know each other. But that can easily turn into an exclusive relationship that cuts out friends and family. Don't let this happen. In cutting others out, you not only hurt people who love you, but you open the door to becoming a wolf. As Proverbs 15:22 reminds us, "Without counsel plans fail, but with many advisers they succeed."

Three-Corded Love

One strand is easily broken. Two strands are better than one because if one breaks, the other is there to take on the weight. But a three-corded piece of rope? That's strength.

When Brittney and I were going through a very difficult time in our relationship, she chose three cords, and I chose one.

People prayed for Brittney. She was able to express her innermost feelings, thereby releasing bottled-up emotions. And others could weep with her in her weeping.

Me, on the other hand…I bottled up my feelings, cried silently in my room, pressed my fingernails into my skin, and tried to drown out the wailing in my soul.

And what eventually brought me out of it? A friend who pursued me week after week, even when I didn't want to be pursued.

It's humbling to let others hold you up when you feel you can continue alone, but the hit to your pride is a small blow for the strength you'll radiate in your relationship. So humble yourself. Open your relationship to those who love you and want what's best for you. Get vulnerable. Ask for help and advice and lots of specific prayer. This is usually an honor for others.

If your relationship means enough to you that you want to give it every last ounce of your strength, why not recruit the willing strength of others?

A CORD OF THREE STRANDS

One Cord: Just You. When entering a relationship, you can have all sorts of resolutions and willpower. But the fact is, no one can stay strong forever. We all break. And when our one cord breaks, everything falls apart—and trying to tie it back together is a long, tedious process. I chose this way with Brittney at first because I thought I could handle it. It didn't take long before failure humbled me and I realized that there was no way I could fly without help.

Two Cords: You and Another. Having the support of another in your relationship is huge. This person can be there to talk with you through your feelings and your struggles and also push you to stick to your convictions. For much of my relationship with Brittney, this person was my pastor, who not only left his office door open to me but actually sought me out and urged me to choose what was best.

Three Cords: You, Another, and a Tribe of Loved Ones. Opening your relationship to several people who love you allows you to be bolstered with prayer, encouragement, and support. The older I get, the more I experience the amazing power of Christian community and prayer. We may never understand how it all works, but God has clearly shown us in Scripture that these aspects play a beautiful role in his economy. Find people to pray for you and your relationship, and be specific in your requests.

The Responsibility Is Yours

Even if you're great at controlling your physical urges, harnessing your tongue, and responding rightly to inner alarms, it doesn't mean much if you freely allow your other to make advances on you.

One of the most loving things Brittney ever did for me was confront me about my advances toward her. I still remember the words she said and the follow-up letter she wrote me. It hurt like crazy to see how terribly I'd gone against God, forced the love of my life into a difficult situation, and been too weak to show the same tough love my sweetheart had shown me.

But some hurt is good. And this was very good hurt.

Relationships are where marital principles start to take form. And the whole aim of marriage is to love each other as Jesus loves—to give each other one hundred percent of your love even when the other is not reciprocating.

You need to take one hundred percent of the responsibility in your physical purity—even when your other is making it difficult.

If your other suddenly becomes weak-willed, it doesn't give you freedom to go along with the poor decisions. Quite the opposite. It gives you an even weightier responsibility to shoulder. It puts you in the hard position of having to hurt your other's pride in order to obey God.

But again, it's a good kind of hurt.

Now, if you've already gone much farther than you ever wanted to go physically, don't think it's too late to right the ship. Will it be difficult? Yes. But it will also be sweet for you and your other. Because your bones will no longer groan with unrepentant sin. It's never too late to give your physical sin to Jesus. But at the same time, it's never too early, either. Don't keep on living in guilt-ridden pleasure just because you're planning on getting married. Put an end to it. Build moats. Respond to your alarms. Pursue a three-cord relationship. Marriage isn't a technicality with God. It's sacred. And he commands that we stay pure until that day.

A Reason for Purity

The decision to remain physically pure isn't for some half-baked, because-I'm-a-Christian reason. Nor should it be viewed as the secret ingredient to an amazing relationship or the ticket to a great sex life in marriage. The whole point of staying pure is to obey God both in heart and in body—and to do things his way.

It just so happens that his way is also the best way (a fact supported by secular research). Keeping yourself pure until marriage—originally or from this day forward—esteems God's grand design, infuses nobility and discipline into other areas of your life, and empowers you to love in ways that are otherwise unattainable. It makes possible the kind of companionship, conversation, sex, and emotional wholeness that most want but no one thinks is real. It's a huge part of achieving the meaningfulness God designed for every day after the wedding day.

The wedding is so much more wondrous. It celebrates the beautiful conversion from fragmented to whole and marks the beginning of you and your other as one. It culminates in a stunning portrait of trust, respect, and a deep knowing of one another that no one else can ever touch.

It brings all of the abstract symbolism of marriage into a tangible, transcendent expression. You selflessly, vulnerably, and fully give your body and heart to your other because it's actually intact. And this expression doesn't end after the honeymoon. It begins on the honeymoon and carries on through your lifetime.

> Some acts of sexuality reflect the deep knowing and mutual respecting God intended. Others are nothing more than a physical act. And that's just not enough.
>
> Dannah Gresh[10]

God's way isn't just difficult for difficulty's sake. It's beautiful and pure for his sake and ours. He doesn't just bless purity. He built it into the DNA of fully experiencing love. I like how Dannah Gresh puts it: "As God looks upon humanity, groaning to communicate His love, He wants to direct our attention to a portrait that comes close to helping us understand. That portrait is a pure, holy marriage."[11]

Mark Driscoll shares these statistics about couples who marry as virgins:[12]

- Men who marry as virgins are 37 percent less likely to divorce.
- Women who marry as virgins are 24 percent less likely to divorce.
- Those who wait to have sex until marriage and remain faithful in marriage report higher levels of life satisfaction compared to adults who engage in premarital or adulterous sex.
- Those who wait to have sex and are faithful to their spouse also report notably higher happiness scores.

Saving Your Other from Yourself Doesn't Rob You of Joy—It Amplifies It

Aside from craving physical pleasure, many rush into sexual activity because they feel as though they'd be missing out if they didn't.

Nothing could be further from the truth.

Protecting the purity of your other—and, in turn, protecting yours—doesn't rob you of physical experiences. When you fight for purity and reach the altar whole, you don't find a pile of *Wish We Hads*. Instead, you find eager anticipation.

I'm not saying that purity guarantees amazing sex (though it certainly helps). But it does signify the fulfillment of God's perfect design, which manifests itself in ways that are so much more brilliant and deeper than the physical act of sex.

Though virgins, Brittney and I arrived on our wedding day with a list of regrets. We took our physical relationship too far, which often cast a dark cloud of guilt and pain over us. But we never stopped fighting for purity because we knew that God's design brings blessings, not hurts. And we can confidently say that the blessings are worth the temporary difficulty. Really worth it.

> There is a right way, there is a best way, and it is the same way: God's way (1 Thessalonians 4:3-8). God did not give us rules just to steal all of our fun; he's called us to holiness, and the rules are for our joy and protection.
>
> Brandon Andersen[13]

The world will tell you it's a good thing to experience physical intimacy. It will mockingly smile and laugh, *Why wait*? It will say you take God too seriously. It will say that you're missing out.

Don't buy into these lies. The world is blind and deaf to the wondrous design of our King. So fight for purity. Pray for success. Protect each other as though you were guarding a lifelong investment.

Because that's exactly what you're guarding.

What's Next

Everyone has a certain persona and uniqueness. But all too often we guard it, afraid of what others will think. In the next chapter, we're going to explore how to free one another to be the person God created us to be.

Ask Those Who Fly

What steps did you take in the fight to remain pure? Was it effective or not? Explain.

We tried to make rules. And didn't follow them…at least for long. We tried to get accountability…it wasn't consistent. This was a big area of failure for us. Although we entered marriage technically virgins, we definitely messed up a lot.

Kaisha

Purity comes from a love for God and his design for emotional intimacy and sexuality. For us, our shared desire was to honor God by reserving the sexual delight he designed into our bodies and relationship for after we had made the lifelong commitment of marriage. Saving sex for the *One* has made it incredibly more deep, hilarious, and fun. There's no second-guessing, worries of comparisons, or secrets. I'm hers and she's mine.

Josh

We asked for accountability from our parents and set clear, defined boundaries on what we would and wouldn't do before getting married. The boundaries did help us avoid many temptations, but it was definitely our own walks with the Lord that determined how strong we would be each time we were together. We found that purity is first an attitude of the heart and needed to be nurtured from there first.

Kyle & Corina

We made sure that we were never alone in a house together so as to remove unnecessary temptation. We didn't get into situations where our integrity could be compromised or questioned. The result was a pure relationship where the other person's best interests were elevated above self. If, for some reason, the relationship didn't work out, we knew that we were blameless before the Lord and the other person's future spouse. There's comfort in that approach.

Matt

Though neither of us believes that kissing before marriage is necessarily wrong, it was a decision Isaac had made long before he met me as a line he refused to cross until marriage. He, having examined himself, saw this to be one of the best ways to keep himself pure both physically and mentally. Though I believe there is no one-size-fits-all set of rules for purity, every couple should have them. They should all be rooted first in obedience to God and second in the valuing of one another. They not only serve as physical fences that are easier to see, but they remind us that physical intimacy is not bad or sinful in and of itself; it is something blessed that God has saved for the bonds of marriage.

Melissa

In our relationship we talked about and set boundaries pretty early on. We laid out where we wanted the lines to be drawn and made sure we were on the same page. Was this effective? In some cases yes because when things started heading in the wrong direction, the boundaries were quick to come to mind. Your conscience is a very strong reminder in times of temptation. But the devil is strong, and if you listen to him telling you that temporary pleasure is better than following God's command for purity, boundaries are quick to be compromised.

Troy & Bailey

What kind of supporting cast did you have— and how helpful was it?

I had several pastors and mentors that I could confide in. It was very helpful! If you don't have someone you can tell what's going on and confess to, you're a lot less likely to repent and walk in the freedom and victory we have in Christ who conquered sin. If Christ has forgiven us we are not bound to the shame of sin, so when we choose to give way to the lie that our sin is too ugly and embarrassing to reveal to another person, we are not believing the gospel.

Jeff

We had a couple friends we confided our struggles in. But it's a very difficult thing to find consistent and unrelenting accountability. There was a point when it went much too far and I confessed to my mom, but she too didn't keep us accountable after that...trying not to be the nosy mother. I should have asked her to please, please be a nosy mother. Real mentors were very hard for us to find.

Kaisha

Family was our biggest support group. The key to their support was that they were on board with our decisions and respected them. While it took humility to allow ourselves to be accountable to our parents, the blessings that resulted were a clean conscience and a strong relationship.

Kyle & Corina

Both sets of our parents were instrumental in orchestrating and supporting our boundaries. In certain moments they warned us that we needed to be more careful, and in others they offered their encouragement and advice. Isaac also had a prayer partner who held him accountable. This, for us, was very helpful.

Melissa

We had a few sets of friends checking in on us, but they were all in the same stage of life and that made it hard. It would have been great to have a young married couple who could explain the aspects of a physical relationship from a godly perspective. Not many people are open about sex. We need it to be a more common conversation, especially in the dating stage of life.

Aaron & Jen

What would you do differently to protect your purity?

I wish we had laid down rules in the beginning and followed them like law. As the relationship progresses it only gets harder. It's so easy to make the excuse that, "Well, I'm going to marry him anyway so it doesn't really matter." But it does matter.

Kaisha

The importance of a closer walk with Christ and daily recommitment to purity can never be overstated to further protect one's emotional purity. On the other hand, if the boundaries become overbearing we would adjust them to avoid frustrating either of us in the relationship.

Kyle & Corina

We were both virgins when we got married, but there were definitely temptations along the way. It's important to cultivate a long-term perspective from the very beginning, and understand the potential damage that one selfish act can cause.

Matt & Jessi

We were rarely alone, unless we were in public places. Being so young and seeing the types of temptations our friends were already falling into, we wanted to be extra careful. It definitely took a lot of self-control and wise decision-making, but it was effective and well worth it for us. Sometimes I felt alone in the fight for purity, especially since most of my friends didn't care about it. Try to find someone who shares your values and ask them to hold you accountable.

Tayler

If we could do it over again we would find friends who were married and ask them to keep us accountable for our purity. This way we would have someone that wasn't our parents asking us about our purity and not taking "we are doing fine" for an answer. We needed someone to really demand the full story and be able to challenge and motivate us through prayer and encouragement. Knowing that once a week someone is going to ask for the details about your purity and having the support of their prayers would have been very beneficial. Another thing we would do differently is take specific time to pray together about our purity. Spending time with God helps us acknowledge our weakness. We can't fight temptation in our own strength.

Troy & Bailey

 How would you encourage someone who wants a God-glorifying relationship but feels physically or emotionally shattered from their broken past?

Have a good understanding of godly grace. If the past is something the other is going to hold over your head and hinder the relationship, it will be a problem. Or if it's something you can't get over, it will cause problems in the relationship.

Jake & Sarah

Every Christian has been rescued by Jesus from spiritual depravity and deadness. Nobody brings anything to the table of life, but instead receives all good things from God (James 1). God is in the business of taking terrible pasts and transforming them into redeemed futures. Nothing a person has done in their past can prevent them from receiving God's mercy, forgiveness, and restoration in their future. Old habits die hard, and the only way to truly change is with the Holy Spirit's power.

Josh

Understand the true nature of forgiveness and your worth and value to God. Jesus died to bring about forgiveness and restoration. This communicates a person's inestimable worth to the Father.

Matt

Seek God. He is Jehovah-Rapha, the Healer, and he binds up the wounds of the brokenhearted. Ask him to guide your steps as you seek to honor him with a relationship. Likely, it will be harder than other relationships, and unique trials may have to be overcome. But we remember that what was intended for evil can be used for good with God. And difficult times are often used to refine us, though that's not comforting to hear in the midst of them. When your past rears its ugly head, the King of Kings is there with you. You have the power of the Living God inside you. There is nothing that cannot be overcome, for your Father loves you fiercely, and his hands are infinitely gentle with those who are broken.

Melissa

7

WHAT MANY MISS OUT ON

*One way God establishes beauty is by putting
things that are different next to each other.*

PAUL DAVID TRIPP

*I*magine standing in a desert filled with what looks like rocks from a distance. But as you get closer, you realize these rocks are actually the tops of buried statues. They all look the same to you because you can only see a fraction of what's actually there.

Now, grab a shovel. Start digging.

What you soon discover is these statues aren't all alike. Not even close. Some resemble your own height, weight, and frame. Others are polar opposites of you. Some seem warmly familiar. Others give you the creeps. The one thing the statues have in common is they are solid. Unmovable. Whoever designed them obviously didn't want anyone coming along and changing them—no matter how wonderful or offensive they are to you.

In your relationship with your other, there will be a desire in you to change something non-sinful about him or her. Something that's rooted in their God-given makeup, their unique design. And if you're going to give what's needed over what you want, you need to accept your other's differences—and, if at all possible, admire and adore them.

You may be tempted to shrug off this chapter because you love everything about your other. Don't. As your relationship deepens, more differences will surface. At first, you may find them quirky or cute. But over time you might find yourself equating "different" with "wrong." You might consciously or subconsciously think that you are better because your other processes emotions differently, approaches conflicts differently, or simply washes the dishes differently.

It's something God really needed to change about me when I first started dating Brittney.

From the moment we started getting to know each other, the more pronounced our differences became. She lived in the moment; I lived in light of the bigger picture. She wore her heart on her sleeve; I worried about what others thought of my words and actions. She was more laid-back; I was more responsible.

The person may not seem to be on the same track, but she may have a much deeper track that you can't see because of your own issues. Do not assume, for example, that because she does not know the Bible as well as you that she does not love God as much as you.

Henry Cloud
and John Townsend[1]

We had a choice to either delight in these differences or try to change each other. This chapter helps you do the former—which isn't always easy, but God clearly commands it.

The apostle Paul writes that we who trust in Jesus are a part of one body and the fullness of Christ. We don't have the same function—but instead radically different ones that God specifically created for each of us (Romans 12:3-5). These unique functions are intimately tied to God's design of our personalities, perspectives, and quirks. When we refuse to appreciate, or at the very least accept, our other's differences, we refuse a part of God's handiwork that he established for his good purposes.

So it makes perfect sense that we should embrace the functions of others—even those that seem strangely different from us. If you love your other but find yourself wanting to change part of his or her makeup, it's time for you to chew on two truths: (1) Trying to change God's good creation is wrong and (2) simply tolerating his creation isn't a formula for success.

Marry someone you want to be married to for the rest of your life, not someone you hope to transform into a satisfactory spouse in five years' time.

Gary Thomas[2]

You need to re-hardwire the way you see differences in order to build a thriving relationship.

Differences Are Beauty to Delight In

To view your other's differences as annoyances would be tragic. Differences aren't just some hindrance to be dealt with. They're a beauty to delight in.

You might surprise yourself when you come to adore your other's differences. Things that ordinarily annoy you become a source of appreciation for God's unique design. Slowly but steadily you become a more balanced person because of the influence your other has on you.

I saw this firsthand in Brittney's parents.

Brittney's mom would be sharing a story at the dinner table that didn't exactly fascinate the kids, but Brittney's dad would be glued to her every word. He'd get out of his chair, kiss her, and say, "You are so darn cute!"

Instead of mentally checking out, he adored how different she was from him. He loved watching her eyes get big and her hand motions get wild as she told a story.

My relationship with Brittney is better today because of how her dad relates to her mom. It seems now that everything I adore most about Brittney is the exact opposite of me!

While I speak sparingly, she delights in telling elaborate, detailed stories—whether or not they're what you might call memorable. And, just like her dad, I find great joy in that. I can't help but grin like an idiot sometimes as she walks me through the events of her day.

A second difference I've come to appreciate so much in Brittney is her perspective on what's really important. Things that would justifiably upset most people—a family member cracking your phone or dinging your car—roll off her back because she cares so much more for people than things. I love that about her. But it's a choice. I could just as easily be frustrated that she would care so little for the damage of expensive possessions.

This appreciation of differences goes both ways for us.

Most of my quirks—making up words, buying cheap stuff that usually breaks in a day, locking the car no matter how safe the location is, tapping on anything to create music—she has come to love about me. She might not always like them, but they're things she misses when I stop. Sometimes out of nowhere she mimics one of my weird traits and we both bust a gut.

These things make me feel accepted and loved, and she knows this.

Ask yourself: *Is my other more logically or emotionally inclined? Carefree or calculated? An introvert or an extrovert? Happy-go-lucky or reserved?*

> Our differences, accepted and appreciated, are God's way of making us fit together as a couple so that we will be stronger together than either of us could be apart.
>
> Jack and Carole Mayhall[3]

None of these answers are wrong or inferior. They're just different. You can either (1) refuse to understand your differences, determining that they are wrong and you are right; (2) merely tolerate their differences, silently critiquing and criticizing them in your heart; or (3) delight in their differences, recognizing that God created each one for a specific purpose, maybe even to make you a better person.

Among these choices, it's easy to see which one will create the most unity in your relationship. By delighting in your other's differences, you're not only strengthening your love for each other, you're becoming more like Jesus.

Differences Make You More Like Jesus

I grew up as the youngest of three boys. I loved roughhousing with my brothers and was very competitive. Brittney grew up as the oldest of five (three girls, two boys), used her imagination to create fun, and loved taking care of her younger siblings.

When Brittney and I started dating, I became the older brother to her two little brothers who were both under six. I loved it. But it didn't take long to see differences in the way Brittney treated her brothers and the way I treated them.

One day while we were playing backyard baseball, I found myself getting frustrated with the older brother because he was demanding that the game be played his way. On top of that, the younger brother was goofing off despite my warning for him to stand back so he wouldn't get hurt.

I barked at the older, telling him what my older brothers would've done to me if I'd mouthed off like he had. Soon after, the younger got hurt because he wasn't paying attention to the ball.

The way I grew up, it would've been normal to snub the disrespectful brother until he showed some respect and then turn around and tell the younger one *I told you so.*

It makes me sad now to think about it.

Brittney was different.

When the younger brother started to cry from getting hit with the ball, she ran up to him right away, picked him up, and kissed his cheeks. I could tell something was upsetting her.

"What's wrong?" I asked, when the game was over.

She told me she didn't like the way I had talked to the older brother. She explained that although his behavior was disrespectful, underneath were leadership qualities in need of shaping.

She continued: "Say a group of kids are playing and one kid becomes terribly bossy and starts taking control of the game. You don't want to bash him so that he never leads again. You need the grace to see that he hasn't arrived yet, and that the process of eliminating the sin and learning to lead is long—and one you can help him with. Right now, you only see the sin. But try to see the eighteen-year-old he'll be someday and shape him toward that."

That day marked the start of some profound changes in my life.

Brittney showed me that grace is not only giving someone what they don't deserve—such as mentorship to the older brother and compassion to the younger—but also extends genuine love. This meant being patient and kind toward her brothers and choosing to disciple them without falling into irritableness or resentfulness.

Brittney's compassion and grace toward her brothers began a process of transformation in me—a process that moved me from heartless criticism and resentment to a passionate desire to mentor young souls. This is one of the most amazing truths about differences: They help us mirror Christ and show us that some of the things we consider normal are not normal at all in the eyes of Jesus.

Start observing your other's differences and you just might discover things about yourself that need to change.

Differences Point Toward Purpose

I'll never forget the look on my English tutor's face when she tested me at the beginning of the school year. Mildred was her name. She was old enough to be my great-grandma, and she always wore the same blue dress.

First, she tested me on my spelling ability. What a horrible place to start. I couldn't even spell *fail*. Her face hardened, realizing just how much work I'd be.

Next, she tested my handwriting—which seemed irrelevant because wasn't that what computers were for? But in her mind it was 1930-something. She laughed at what I'd written and said my paper looked like a third grader's scribbles. Mind you, I was fourteen. This made me feel like garbage.

Finally, she tested reading comprehension. I remember thinking, *What does comprehension mean?* But before I knew it she began reading sections from a book and asking me questions. With each question I answered, Mildred's eyes grew brighter and brighter. When I answered the final question, she snapped the book closed and triumphantly announced, "You tested out of college in reading comprehension!"

I became someone new that day.

Without even knowing it, Mildred helped me discover a skill I didn't even know existed. From then on I went to class with hope and confidence. Not even my third-grade handwriting could get me down.

We're often blind to our differences until someone points them out in a positive way. When this happens, we begin to see them as our gift. And with this gift, we find our purpose. We "serve one another, as good stewards of God's varied grace…in order that in everything God may be glorified through Jesus Christ" (1 Peter 4:10-11).

In your relationship, help your other discover his or her differences in a positive light. Pay attention to what strikes you about your other's personality traits, abilities, and passions. Look for patterns in how he or she affects the people around them. Then when the time is right, express your thoughts about it. Don't be aggressive, as if you know God's plan for him or her. Just share what you've observed and say something like, "I wonder how God will use _____ in your life." Then let it simmer. Wait a few weeks before revisiting the conversation. In doing so, you just might help unearth their God-given purpose.

> Having gifts that differ according to the grace given to us, let us use them: if prophecy, in proportion to our faith; if service, in our serving; the one who teaches, in his teaching; the one who exhorts, in his exhortation; the one who contributes, in generosity; the one who leads, with zeal; the one who does acts of mercy, with cheerfulness (Romans 12:6-8).

How to Delight in Differences

To truly delight in your other's differences, you need to embrace the three traits of flying: selflessness, vulnerability, and transcendence. Selflessness takes the focus off of you and puts it on him or her. Vulnerability requires that you open yourself up to being changed by those differences. And transcendence turns tolerance into delight.

First, pinpoint all the ways your other is different from you. In one row, write down the differences you admire and adore about him or her. In the second row, write down the differences you accept or tolerate. And in the third row, write down how your other is different from you in a way you don't understand or even makes you angry or moody. If nothing comes to you, ask yourself: *When was the last time my other did something or said something that annoyed me? When was the last time he/she did something that made me feel uncomfortable or awkward?* Write that down.

DIFFERENCES I ADORE

DIFFERENCES I TOLERATE

DIFFERENCES THAT ANGER ME

Now ask yourself how you might go about moving the things you listed in row three into row two, and row two into row one. Get humble. Kill whatever pride may be festering in you. Ask yourself: *In what ways can I delight in the beauty of his/her differences? How might my other's differences change me for the better?*

Sometimes you'll find that you simply cannot delight in a difference. You'll discover that tolerance is as far as you can push the needle. If this is the case, it's not a deal-breaker unless you're constantly falling into sin because of your other's non-sinful differences. At that point, you need to consider ending the relationship. Not because your other has done anything wrong, but because you're just not compatible.

> Unity is not the result of sameness. Rather, unity results when love intersects with difference.
>
> Paul David Tripp[4]

Jesus Makes Our Differences Perfect

John the Baptist had his differences. He spent a ton of his life in the wilderness. Ate honey crushed from dates. Ground the bean of the locust tree for flour and bread. And he probably reeked of dirt and grime.

But "among those born of women there has arisen no one greater than John the Baptist" (Matthew 11:11). And he was "great before the Lord" (Luke 1:15).

God knew John while he was in his mother's womb. He filled him with his Spirit before he'd even opened his eyes. The Lord had a great plan for John the Baptist: to pave the way for the ministry of Jesus. But this plan meant he'd live a strange life, set apart from what was normal. God gifted John with specific differences for the purpose of completing his plan.

In a similar way, God has known you and your other since before your births. And he has a great plan for both of you: to make disciples until Christ's return.

Some of us teach, some of us evangelize. Some of us serve, some of us encourage. Each of these differences are given by God to equip you. Embrace them. Delight in them. And always remember: No matter how polar opposite your differences are, Jesus promises that he is in the process of conforming you into his image.

In other words, you are perfect exactly how God made you. And so is your other.

> And we all, with unveiled face, beholding the glory of the Lord, are being transformed into the same image from one degree of glory to another. For this comes from the Lord who is the Spirit (2 Corinthians 3:18).

What's Next

You and your other have to truly know each other before your relationship can progress. The next chapter gives you the tools to do just that.

Ask Those Who Fly

What kind of differences have you learned to not only accept about your other, but love about him or her?

Andrew is very laid-back and easy going and rarely gets visibly excited about anything, while I get excited about everything and am very up-and-down with my mood and emotions. These two extremes are things we have chosen to enjoy about each other, rather than find annoying. We balance each other out. I keep life exciting while Andrew keeps the family stable.

Andrew & Abigail

Cody is very assertive. And I'm not. We are like night and day. He's opinionated, passionate, and has no problem making decisions, planning, and voicing his preferences. He's a natural leader and doesn't let people take advantage of him. I go with the flow. I'm a follower. I do things last-minute and don't really plan anything. I hate confrontation and avoid having preferences so I don't offend anybody. The difference in Cody attracts me to him. I knew that I needed someone like him. You just can't have two people saying, "Well, I just want to do what you want to do" all the time.

Kaisha

Almost one hundred percent of the time, I love that Jake is much more spontaneous than me. We go on way more adventures, and probably have way more fun than if it were just me making the decisions. He helps push me out of my comfort zone a little bit, but really, he is my comfort zone. So as long as he's by my side, I'll go on any adventure. Our kids will probably have a much more memorable childhood because of him too. And I love that.

Sarah

While I tend to be much more spontaneous, odds are, some details have been overlooked. Sarah is much more detail-oriented and likes to plan ahead. Most of the time, this means that my "great ideas" can be more successful because she makes sure it happens at the right time and with the right supplies.

Jake

Kristi approaches life in a fundamentally different way. She's a Mac and I'm a PC, as it were. She is tremendously more emotive than I, and her expressions of emotion have a completely different meaning than if I'd uttered the same words. I also appreciate that Kristi isn't as ambitious as I am. If both of us were competing as I do, our relationship would be pulled apart. I increasingly appreciate her contentment and lack of desire to *win*.

Josh

Kyle was a really quiet guy when I met him. I knew I'd probably marry a quieter type but now I had to really get used to the idea! Over our courtship I grew to deeply appreciate that his quietness also reflected a quietness of heart. He didn't have to be the center of attention, didn't have to complain about his day, and didn't have to tell the world about his talents and abilities in order to feel heard. His security was in Christ.

Corina

Jessi is practical; I am not. She's a realist, a meticulous planner, and cautious. I'm the opposite of each of them. And rather than being intimidated, irritated, or frustrated, I understand that my other provides balance. She strengthens me where I'm blind or weak, and I do the same for her via my strengths. The blessing comes in realizing that and utilizing the other's strengths. It's about teamwork!

Matt

Isaac is a rock who often sees things in only black and white. And while this was very hard at times, I came to see that his personality was a good balance for our marriage. We complemented each other because we each leaned toward a different extreme. Isaac is very strong in his opinions and steadfast in his beliefs. He balances me out when my faith wavers and I am uncertain. On the other hand, I am softer and tend to think about things from all sides of the equation. I balance out his rigidity and soften his hard thinking.

Melissa

I'm high-strung, and Kyle is not. In fact, he's so mellow and laid-back that sometimes I'm tempted to check his pulse just to make sure he's still breathing. At first, this really frustrated me. When I was feeling upset or angry and he didn't get as worked up as me, I felt like he didn't care. However, I've come to learn that he's just better at rolling with the punches than I am. This is great for me. He balances me out and calms me down when I'm in freak-out mode over something miniscule.

Tayler

It blesses me that Jeff is willing to talk openly about theology. When we first started dating, we wondered how our theological differences would affect us over the long haul, but it has actually served as a bit of spice to the relationship. I find that I'm challenged and convicted of being narrow or judgmental where it might not be evident if I were in a relationship with someone who has the same views as me. And yet throughout those conversations there is a high degree of safety and a strong foundation on the gospel.

Heather

What differences have you simply had to learn to accept?

I'm I saver, Corina's a spender. I'd like to say that I exhibit the better of the two qualities, but that's not necessarily true. She has a carefree and live-to-the-fullest personality that I love. She adds the spark to my life. While I still love to save, I'm fine with seeing her love to spend.

Kyle

We value different things. What's important to me isn't necessarily so to her. But there's understanding even in disagreement. The key is individual humility. I have to realize that God gave me this woman for several reasons, and one of them is to provide a different way of thinking about our family's situation, future, and direction. Disagreements become easier to accept when we realize that we (individually) don't have it all figured out.

Matt

Something that I have learned to accept but that I am still not crazy about is that Troy is not good at relaxing or just taking a day to do nothing. If there is an hour left in the day Troy will make sure that none of it is wasted. He is a worker bee, which isn't a bad thing but gets a little old when he can never just stop and do nothing. If I want to spend quality time with him I usually have to help with his projects or whatever he is working on for that evening or weekend. I have learned that this is who he is and that I am not going to change him. It is better to go along with it than let it get me frustrated.

Bailey

When Tyler and I are in a stressful or tricky situation, he needs to concentrate in quietness and solve the problem at hand. I found that confusing because I talk problems out and would try to do so, only making matters more stressful for him. I've learned to accept his way of solving problems.

Jen

 How have your other's differences changed you for the better?

Andrew's ability to roll with the punches has encouraged me to work on being easier going and more flexible when plans change. Slowly, I've grown in this area due to his influence and example.

Abigail

Kyle's calmer personality helps quiet my fiery emotions every day. When I feel like shouting about my latest misery, Kyle's influence helps me turn my burdens over to the Lord in prayer. He balances me out.

Corina

I eat better—a huge plus! I'm more cautious and thoughtful in making big decisions. I've started writing lists and have become more organized. I see my own shortcomings more clearly—things (even sin) that were blind spots to me previously.

Matt

Kyle has truly inspired me to put my trust in God no matter what. Many times his mellow demeanor isn't him "not caring," but him trusting that God will carry us through. I usually try to take things into my own hands, and he encourages me to release them into God's hands instead.

Tayler

Jen puts my mind to work. Sometimes I feel like just ignoring a situation or question but she pushes me to address the problem and come to a solution that is good for both of us. She is my mental workout.

Tyler

8

HOW TO KNOW AND BE KNOWN

The truth is, we want to be known; we truly do. But we're afraid. If you see the real me, will you run away? Am I even worth being known? Will the real me bore you? Scare you? Repulse you? And so we…aim to get them to like us, rather than intentionally help them to truly understand us.

GARY THOMAS

*W*hen U.S. airports installed full-body scanners at security checkpoints, Americans got vocal about the revealing photos, complaining that it was a violation of privacy. In fact, everyone made such an uproar that a few years later, the TSA replaced the full-body scanners with scanners that only showed generic images, flushing millions of dollars in the process.

We'll make sacrifices for the sake of safety in our country, but at the end of the day, we don't want people seeing us naked.

The same is true of our souls.

Yes, we yearn for our other to know us wholeheartedly. But the risk of rejection is often too great. So instead, we reveal only our commendable traits and bury our scars and secrets deep inside us. It's a best-foot-forward mentality that severely hinders honesty, trust, and open communication in a relationship.

This needs to change. Because if your other doesn't fully know you, the relationship will never progress into what God intends it to be.

This is where soul scanning comes in.

Soul Scanning

Soul scanning involves being real about your past, present, and future. It's about creating a holistic picture of how God has shaped you up to this point.

Your other knows only so much about you when you start a relationship. As you both become closer, it's important to intentionally reveal more and more of your soul. Not just the stuff you're proud of, but the stuff you're struggling with or working on too.

In order to be known—to give what your other needs most—you need to learn the careful art of revealing the essence of who you are.

A soul scan encourages transparency in all things: your goals, hobbies, quirks, habits, passions, personal beliefs, and even past regrets, when told in the right setting. Soul scans make transparent everything from your love of sports to the abuse you may have suffered as a child.

But be cautious. Feel out the status of the relationship before you bear your soul. It should go without saying that soul scanning on a first date would most likely be disastrous.

Soul scanning isn't a license to reveal everything about yourself that your other might not be ready for. It's simply about showing your other the true you so that he or she can evaluate whether or not forever makes sense.

God clearly values the integrity that comes with soul scanning. "The LORD detests lying lips, but he delights in people who are trustworthy," says Proverbs 12:22.

Soul scanning makes you honorable before God and your other (2 Corinthians 8:21). It keeps your lips from speaking deceit, which leads to a desirable life and good days on earth (1 Peter 3:10). It makes you the delight of God and saves you from destruction (Proverbs 16:13; Proverbs 11:3). And finally, it practices the Golden Rule of treating your other as you would like to be treated (Luke 6:31). Because no one likes being left in the dark about important issues when *forever* is on the line.

Letting your other peer into your soul helps develop trust and respect—two things you absolutely need for the relationship to thrive.

So let your other travel beyond the walls you've built for yourself. Give them a panoramic view of your soul.

Soul Scanning in Action

Few feelings are more reassuring than knowing that your other knows you completely—even the ugly stuff—and still loves you. But the time to fully know and be known doesn't begin at the altar.

It begins the moment you and your other start a relationship.

> The temptation will be to say what you think the other person wants to hear, but that's setting up both of you for considerable disappointment and even lifelong frustration.
>
> Gary Thomas[1]

After being separated for two and a half years, Brittney and I had some serious catching up to do when we finally got back together. We have sweet memories of these talks—swaying on the porch swing in the summer and sipping coffee on the couch in the winter.

Though it mostly happened subconsciously, I revealed seven important things about myself to Brittney. The first three are in the green category because they're the easiest for most of us. The next three are yellow because many of us get timid when it comes to expressing our values and beliefs. The last is red because we must approach it with care.

GREEN

- Interests
- Goals
- Habits

YELLOW

- Values
- Beliefs
- Life Vision

RED

- Mistakes

Green

Interests

As a sports journalist, I revealed my love for writing and professional athletics. The writing part made sense to Brittney. She adored writing and seemed to fill up journals and notebooks in her sleep. She wasn't really sure what to do with the sports, though—she could only name one or two professional athletes on a good day. But she graciously accepted sports as a part of who I am and watched many games with me even though she would've rather watched paint dry. And no, that's not much of an exaggeration!

Goals

Goals can be tricky because they often change. The best thing you can do is to get to the root of your goals—their point of origin. For me, that point was to use my gift of writing in both vocation and ministry. The vocation part seemed clear early in our relationship. I would earn a living as a journalist. But it wasn't until we were engaged that God began prodding me to write for him. Brittney vividly remembers the winter day I told her I wanted to write a book for believers. Although it scared her, she accepted my goal, believing that God had his hand in my life.

Habits

Everyone has weird habits and quirks. It's just a matter of whether or not you recognize them. If you don't, your other will. And that's a good thing. It allows him or her to discover what they're getting into. I like dancing like a dork, doing improv, making funny voices, and goofing off in general. The thought of acting like that in front of Brittney embarrassed me at first. But once I did, I realized she was falling deeper in love with me. The real me. And that's the whole point of revealing yourself through soul scanning. You want your other to embrace the true you, not some blurred version of you.

Yellow

Values

Because Brittney and I grew up in the same church, it was relatively easy to reveal my values to her. We both valued a relationship with Jesus, treasured the Word of God, and loved investing time into family and the body of Christ. Even so, we differed on scriptural gray areas and various aspects of everyday life. For example, she valued time with her sisters while I valued time with friends outside of my family. Certain values like this might appear harmless, but you need to discuss them in order to avoid trouble.

Beliefs

Again, attending the same church helped immensely. We didn't need to reveal much in terms of what we thought about God, how we interpreted his Word, and what it meant for our lives. But that didn't stop us from talking a ton about our beliefs. It's one thing to hear the same things from a pulpit. It's another to embrace those words in your heart and reflect them in your everyday life together. The more you discuss your beliefs with your other, the better.

Life Vision

Life vision is what you foresee in your future. Do you see kids? How many? Will you eat around a dinner table or in front of the TV? How generous will you be with your money and time? How do you see your God-given gifts translated into everyday life? Do you see yourself cooking meals, your other cooking meals, or tag-teaming? Do you see yourself working forty hours a week, staying at home, going back to school, or going into fulltime ministry? Will weekends be jam-packed with parties and activity, or do you see yourselves relaxing and enjoying the sunset? If God blesses you with kids, what will their path of education look like? Public school, private school, homeschool, or online curriculum? Will you live in the country or in the city? Do you foresee yourself creating your own traditions together or continuing with the ones of your parents? Think you'll attend a bigger church or a smaller one?

Don't let these questions scare you off. You don't need to write essays explaining each answer and why. But you should openly talk about them and express your general feelings so that your other knows exactly where you stand—which hints at the course you'll eventually take.

Red

Mistakes

Pain from your past belongs in the red category because it requires the most care. You don't want to get into a rela-

> Who we are today is a reflection of our past experiences.
>
> H. Norman Wright[2]

tionship and spill all your dirty secrets on the first date. That would belittle the grace and forgiveness of Jesus. That said, you also don't want your other to fall in love with you while you hide past or present sins (i.e. a sexual history, a child out of wedlock, addictions to drugs, porn, alcohol, lying, adultery). Your other deserves to know where you're coming from to determine whether he or she can spend the rest of their life with you. And even though it will hurt your pride—and maybe cost you the relationship—you need to own up to the decisions you've made, believing fully that you are forgiven and loved by Jesus.

Prioritize Full Disclosure

Now it's time to act. I encourage you to slowly and wisely reveal yourself to your other. Though some of your attempts will end in hard discussions or even arguments, you will reap the incredible joy of open communication and mutual understanding.

If I hadn't revealed my passion to write for God, my love of sports, my goofy side, my face-plants, my beliefs, my life vision, and so much more, Brittney wouldn't have fully known who she was committing her life to. For those who consider break-up or divorce a ready option, concealing these things is natural. But as believers, we need to be like Jesus and offer our other total transparency in spite of tension, embarrassment, or wounded pride.

To make transparency a priority in your relationship, below are several questions to help you get to know yourself, which in turn helps you give your other a more accurate depiction of who you are too.

Green

Pinpoint your interests. What could you talk about for hours? What gets your heart beating a little quicker and makes you feel fully alive? What are some things you could see yourself doing for a lifetime?

Pinpoint your goals. What are you working toward today? Why? What kind of doors will open if you achieve it? How does this complement your Jesus-given mission of loving God, loving others, and making disciples of Christ?

Pinpoint your habits. What do you find interesting that no one else finds interesting? What makes you weird, different, or just *off* in the way you do things? Why? What are some things you do every day that few others seem to do? What do your friends and family tease you about most? What are some things that you just can't ever seem to stop doing? What would you be embarrassed of if brought up in front of your other?

Yellow

Pinpoint your values. What is worth dying for? What are some things people say that just stab your heart? What are some difficult things you do just because you believe they're right?

Pinpoint your beliefs. What does Jesus mean to you? What does the Holy Spirit mean to you? What is your identity? How do you view the Bible? What role does it play in your life? Which parts of Scripture are gray to you (that is—areas on which you don't take a specific stance because it doesn't seem like the Bible does)? What concepts do you surrender to God because you simply cannot find the answer?

Pinpoint your life vision. What comes to mind when you visualize the good life? If you could look into your future, what would you hope to see? What is your future other like in this vision? When it comes to the people in this future life, who's doing what—and what's being accomplished?

Red

Pinpoint your mistakes. What are you afraid to tell your other? What haunts you about your past? What addictions have you suffered from? What makes you cry out to God in utter helplessness? What are some things you've only confessed to God?

> Therefore, having put away falsehood, let each one of you speak the truth with his neighbor, for we are members of another (Ephesians 4:25).

Observe Your Other Until You're Convinced

To paint a complete picture of yourself to your other is certainly giving what he or she needs most. But that cannot be where your intentionality stops. You too must be fully convinced that you could spend the rest of your life with this person.

And you can't be convinced without serious observation.

> Discerning someone's character, true values, and suitability for marriage is hard work. It takes time, counsel, and a healthy dose of objective self-doubt and skepticism.
>
> Gary Thomas[3]

But before you get sidetracked creating a checklist, answer one question: *Can you see yourself walking toward Jesus with this person?* That's the main thing you're looking for. The other aspects below are important, but this question is the alpha and omega.

Spend a lot of time on that first question before moving on to these:

- What are your other's interests? Can you see yourself making them a part of your life?

- What are your other's goals? Will you be able to support them enthusiastically?

- What are your other's habits and quirks? Do they make you smile

> Ask questions of anyone you date and store their answers in your memory bank to see if the answers continue to be consistent with their actions. If something appears to be a red flag, confront it and don't let it slide.
>
> H. Norman Wright[4]

or annoy you? Can you live with them until death do you part?

- What does your other value? Does it align with God's values? Can you endorse your other's values, or do they offend you? Does your other genuinely love people—|especially those who appear invisible to everyone else? Is your other aware of his or her faults? Quick to seek forgiveness? A giver more than a taker?

- Does your other talk with God or show adoration for Jesus? How does your other view Scripture? Does he or she love, trust, and obey Jesus? Does his or her relationship with Christ show authenticity? Is there a sense of conviction? Is your other on a mission for God?

- How is your other consciously or unconsciously presenting his or her future to you? Can you see yourself in the vision they have for the rest of their life?

- What has your other revealed about his or her past? Is there anything you're afraid to ask because you're afraid it might be true?

What We All Need

The more we reveal about our truest selves, the more naked we feel. We become known in areas that we'd probably rather conceal.

> You can't love what you don't know. You can't be truly loved if you're not truly known. And the only way to know and be known by another person is to communicate—openly, honestly, sincerely, humbly.
>
> Joshua Harris[5]

But here's the beautiful thing. Jesus died naked on a cross so that we would forever be covered in his grace. He gave us all his righteousness in exchange for all our shame. We are free. Utterly and completely free.

To know and be known.

Remember this as you grow closer in your relationship. Don't try to cover up parts of yourself because you're afraid of what your other might think. Accept the fact that you are who you are today, and that every day you're becoming more like Jesus. The person who accepts you for who you are in Christ today is the kind of person who will make you more like him tomorrow—and that's exactly what we all need.

What's Next

You've got what your other needs you to give. You're ready to save him or her from yourself, embrace differences, and know and be known. But what do you actually do while you're together? That's what we look at next.

Ask Those Who Fly

In what ways did you paint an entire picture of who you are to your other? What steps did you take to be authentic with him or her about the real you?

We observed and interacted with each other in a number of different settings—school, family life, church events, work, etc. We felt it was important to see each other in "real life" as opposed to just on dates. We used a list of potential conflict areas to help spark discussion about topics we might not see the same way. We were very honest and real with each other about our convictions and opinions, and we didn't avoid conflict.

Andrew & Abigail

We had dates that were just the two of us, but we also spent a significant amount of time with each other's friends and families. You can tell a lot about a person by the people they choose to spend their time with. It's also very telling to see where a person came from. We saw each other when we were sick, happy, sad, mad, stressed, and everywhere in between.

Jake & Sarah

Isaac and I found it helpful, especially in the beginning, to share in each other's interests. I introduced him to horseback riding, and he started to teach me how to drive cars with manual transmissions. These moments required one or both of us to be vulnerable as we shared our likes and dislikes and tried to value each other's interests. The more we grew to trust each other, the deeper we were able to open up.

Melissa

Do real-life things that you would do on a regular basis as much as possible. Going to the movies or sitting watching the sunset are great things to do and fun date nights, but making a meal, running errands, or working in the yard are better ways of really finding out the true person.

Bailey

What were some hard things you needed to tell your other about your past?

Isaac and I both spent some time relaying our past relationship experiences and some significant struggles we had dealt with. This honest and open sharing was not always a pleasant subject, but it was an attempt to value and respect each other enough to tell the full truth. We did not do all of this right away and in one sitting, though. We waited for what felt like the appropriate time, when our relationship was mature enough to warrant such vulnerable and personal discussion.

Melissa

I had to open up about my low self-esteem due to being bullied. My classmates had written books filled with hundreds of ways to kill me. I had never opened up to anyone about it, and telling Kyle how scarred I was from that experience was intimidating, but he has been so supportive in my social anxiety and self-esteem struggles.

Tayler

Sexual sin was at the top of my list and tough family dynamics was at the top of hers.

Aaron

In what ways did you study your other as you considered whether or not marriage made sense for you?

I needed to know he could be a strong spiritual leader for not only me, but our family. Spending time with his family and going to church together helped me know he had a strong faith and would be able to take on that role. It was also important that he got along well with my family because they are so important to me. That probably would have been a deal-breaker had he not fit in so well. He was also so great around kids. I knew he would be an amazing dad.

Sarah

The most important thing to me was her walk with the Lord. I wanted to be sure her love for the Lord would be more important than her love for me. I needed to see a solid foundation and that her faith was a priority before I stepped into the role of spiritual leader. It was also important for me to see the way she interacted with other people, especially her female friends. She was so good at "being one of the guys" and hanging out with my friends. But it struck me how genuine she was in her friendships with girlfriends, and how sweet and personable she is.

Jake

We assessed each other's relationship with the Lord, long-term life objectives, desire for kids, emotions, and personality. We wanted our relationship to be about more than something physical or fleeting.

Matt

The very first time Kyle came over to my house, my four-year-old brother kicked him, wrapped his arms around his neck, and swung back and forth as Kyle was trying to walk up the stairs to leave. Kyle, only having one sibling, handled it very well. However, I thought to myself, *Well, he's never coming back*. Much to my surprise, he did! And not only did he come back, but he spent quality time with my (four) younger siblings, always did most of the cleaning up after dinner, and engaged in meaningful conversations with my dad. Through these experiences I was able to see how he would treat our family someday.

Tayler

 ## What made you think you were a good match for each other?

Cody knew he wanted to go to seminary. It was non-negotiable. He was interested in foreign missions, but really wanted to be ready to go wherever God led. This was perfect for me. I wanted travel and change. We shared similar ideas about following Jesus and a lot of the Christian living "hot topics" like money, type of church, children's education, women's roles in the home, etc. This was a huge green light to us. It was also an indicator that we were in similar places in our relationships with God.

Kaisha

We just loved being together. It didn't feel like work to get to know one another. We became best friends so fast, and it was so natural to fall in love and want to spend the rest of our lives together. We laugh at the same stupid jokes, we love to have fun together, and we were quickly able to go deep in our conversations without awkwardness.

Jake & Sarah

I had a list of ten things I wanted in a wife before knowing Corina, and she literally passed the test on each. Some, like not wanting pets in the house, were more like perks than non-negotiables. Others, like her spunk, her spiritual depth, and her femininity were treasures I always wanted. And she had them. Besides her personality traits, I knew there was a spark between us—and that helped seal the deal in my heart.

Kyle

We provided each other with balance, we encouraged one another, and we were (are!) crazy about each other. More than that, we both love the Lord and have agreed that he's our primary pursuit.

Matt

One of the first things that truly attracted me to Isaac, other than the fact that he liked to shoot guns and could dance well, was that he was chivalrous in a rare way. If he knew I was arriving at the swing dance center at night and without my younger brother, he would ask me to call him so that he could come out and walk me inside. Little actions like this spoke volumes to me, because even though I was not his significant other, he was committed to protecting and looking after me as a sister in Christ.

Melissa

She quickly became my best friend. We laughed a lot together, which was so refreshing! We had a good mix of similarities and differences. I could be silly with her and she could tell me all the funny things she saw and experienced throughout her day. I fell in love with her character. She was firm in her convictions yet full of grace for others. I could see in her a sincerity of love and care for the people around her. I saw her serving with the gifts she had. She loved and appreciated me as I was. I never felt insecure or like I needed to change to make her happy, but I wanted to be a better person as a result of being around her. I always left our times looking forward to the next time I would see her.

Jeff

What made you question whether or not the relationship was right for both of you?

In the beginning of our relationship we argued about a myriad of issues that we realized later were really not worth arguing about. For example: how many kids we wanted to have vs. adopt. In the end we realized it didn't matter because we both wanted to have and adopt kids, and how many was not something we really needed to worry about right then. It caused a lot of confusion. We had a really hard time distinguishing between "deal breaker" issues and differences.

Kaisha

We both had beliefs and lifestyle choices that had never been questioned before, at least not by someone we cared about, and this caused us to think hard about whether we were right for each other. We were suddenly faced with the notion of trying to combine two different viewpoints, ideas, and lifestyles. How important was our way of doing things? Were we willing to humble ourselves and compromise? Were there "hills to die on" that would make it impossible to create a future together? Would we be able to create a biblical marriage where Jake saw me as his helpmate and I was able to submit to his role as husband?

Sarah

Jessi had this question about me early on in our relationship. She needed a decision-maker, someone who was strong and willing to lead. I had to learn to be that leader (read: man up!). Once that happened (and it took a few months to work through those issues), she was reassured.

Matt

We found ourselves in some fairly serious discussions about the finer details of how we saw ourselves raising a family, such as homeschooling versus public schooling. Because we had such disagreements at first, we both took a serious step back in which we separately took the situation before God, inquired of him, and asked ourselves if these issues were matters of right versus wrong or like versus dislike. When red flags like this go up in your relationship, it doesn't necessarily indicate the end of the world, but it is a reminder to pause, step back, and do some deeper assessment.

Melissa

9

WHEN YOU'RE TOGETHER

*The reason some of us are such poor specimens of Christianity is
because we have no Almighty Christ. We have Christian attributes
and experiences, but there is no abandonment to Jesus Christ.*

Oswald Chambers

ou are a signpost, an Internet ad, a marketing campaign. The
words you say, the moves you make, the thoughts you express,
the body language you use—all of it is one big display for your
special other, and ultimately the entire world.

The question is: What are you advertising?

Some people create the Plastic Person campaign. They constantly
filter their words, weigh their actions, and smile no matter what, hoping to send the vibe that they've got it all together. They want man's
approval over God's approval. It's not the worst campaign in the world,
and probably beats Seducer or Abuser. But the truth is, all of these cam-
paigns pale in comparison to what God desires for us.

God wants you to make your campaign to glorify his Son. He
wants your signpost—everything you say and do—to point to Jesus
and your actions to mirror the King. This is the only way you can give
your other maximum, transcendent love.

Here's how:

Radiate Scripture

Pointing to Jesus must arise from God's Word. We cannot point to
the Son if we don't know who he is, what he's done, and how he's calling us to live. Don't simply subscribe to a reading plan. Crave his Word

as though it comes from the lips of God, living and active, piercing to the human soul, unbreakable, firm forever, the seed of life shouting of Jesus and hope.

Exude the Way of Jesus

Reading the words without living the message is paralyzing and dangerous. The Pharisees were masters at this. They tirelessly studied Scripture, even memorized large portions of it, but they were too entranced with knowledge to care about living it out, like Jesus did.

We must live out the truth we know. This means actively fighting against sin, humbly absorbing the truth of Jesus, asking God for wisdom, doing good, refusing various lusts, proclaiming the excellencies of Christ, and pursuing faith, love, peace, and righteousness.

Be Vocal

What we talk about reflects our treasure, and where our treasure is so is our heart. If we don't talk about our desire to point to Jesus, our hearts won't be in it. When the opportunity arises, talk to your other about how you want your life—and ultimately your relationship—to point to Jesus. Not just as "good Christians" in the traditional sense (*They take notes during the sermon and tithe ten percent*), but as believers who exude Christ's love (*They love the unlovely, serve those who can't repay them, walk in humility, and selflessly give to others what's needed most*).

> One of the most important prerequisites to dating and marrying is being the right person. This means having your identity firmly rooted in Jesus rather than in your identity as a single person, what the culture says about being single, or what the culture says about marriage.
>
> Mark Driscoll[1]

Pointing to Jesus is difficult. It means making unpopular decisions. But it's God's high calling. It's who we are. We are the light of the world not only to those who don't know Jesus, but also to each other.

The sweetest conversations that Brittney and I share are those fixed on God. Our best talks have come while discussing our devotion to him—or lack thereof.

Don't settle for anything less. Do the hard work of fixing your relationship on God.

Ways to Point to Jesus in Your Relationship

This section isn't here to overwhelm you. It's here to show you how simple truths can help you and your other get closer to God and, in turn, each other. Living out these truths probably won't come naturally, but the blessing of obeying God makes the efforts abundantly worthwhile.

Love Strangers

My parents sold their motorhome to a family from Alaska. But my mom and dad didn't just exchange phone calls and paperwork. They took the time to get to know them. In the process, they discovered that the husband—a coastguard in his thirties—had recently suffered from a botched surgery which left him wheelchair-bound. He had lost his job, couldn't play with his kids, and couldn't help his wife with the heavy lifting. Most devastating of all, he had endured several follow-up surgeries with no results.

When the family picked up the motorhome, my parents invited them to join their big home-cooked dinners, brought them to church, and even offered up the guest rooms for as long as they needed. But the biggest miracle of all was something only God could orchestrate. My parents were able to connect the family with a nerve specialist who had cured my mom of a four-year ailment that had baffled every doctor she had ever visited. The specialist was able to miraculously heal the husband and he's now enjoying the sweetness of normal life again.

When we take time to love others, God is at work in us and through us. Don't get so focused on what's happening between you and your other that you miss the world passing by. Love strangers like Jesus. Be a warm presence to those around you. Thank the barista, be kind to the gas station attendant, chat with the person behind you in line, smile at the joggers passing you on the trail, wave at your neighbor when you're getting your mail. Be genuinely friendly. Chat with people you normally wouldn't and find ways to encourage them. When you see someone you'd rather not interact with, do so anyway. Live as if you've been given eternal life with Jesus. Because you have. As Hebrews 13:16 reminds us, "Do not neglect to do good and to share what you have, for such sacrifices are pleasing to God."

Be Interruptible

My friend was doing volunteer work at our church on a Saturday afternoon when a man approached him wearing shoes wrapped in plastic bags. The man had one request. He wanted new shoes.

My friend, now in seminary, is a servant to the core and chose to be interruptible. Instead of handing the guy some cash, my friend saw the man's odd request as an opportunity to invest in a stranger. He drove the man to Wal-Mart and the two talked in the cab of his truck—for hours. But this wasn't just random chitchat. It turned out that the man with plastic-bag shoes was a believer who lavished the encouragement of Jesus on my soon-to-be-pastor friend.

Afterward, my friend and his wife came to our home and recounted the whole thing, saying, "There was just this fire and intensity in his eyes." When he'd finished, we just kind of stared at each other in a sort of dazed awe. Both of us were thinking the same thing—Hebrews 13:2: "Do not neglect to show hospitality to strangers, for thereby some have entertained angels unawares."

Was the man with plastic bags around his shoes an angel, sent to light a fire under my friend before he headed off to seminary? Only God knows. But it was an encounter that won't ever be forgotten.

These are the experiences we unknowingly neglect when we cease being interruptible.

Jesus made himself perhaps the most interruptible man on earth. Yes, he snuck away to spend time with his Father, to rest, and to always move forward in his mission on earth. But when unexpected surprises arose—like a group of men tearing off a roof above him, or a blind man screaming for mercy, or multitudes clamoring to him for healing—he invested himself in the moment.

Don't despise circumstances that change your plans. Accept them as an invitation to do the work of God. Make it fun for you and your other. Guess what God might be up to. Pray on the spot. Ask him to use the two of you in ways you never expected. Look at spontaneous redirections as blessings waiting to happen.

Take Risks

About three years into my career as a sports journalist, I felt God nudging me to quit. For months, I wrestled with making sense of it, engaging with lots of talks with my wife, friends, and mentors, trying to talk sense into myself.

God doesn't really want me to do this, I'd think. *We'll run out of money. It's too risky.*

But the spiritual vibe that I'd be done with journalism kept getting stronger and stronger as the weeks went by. And not just stronger. Precise. I even told my wife, "I think God is going to do something in mid-March."

When February rolled around, I received a phone call from a friend I hadn't spoken with in over a year. Fittingly, I was covering a basketball game at the time. We caught up for a minute and then he said he had an opportunity I might be interested in. A job that would pay my bills and give me flexibility to work on my writing. Ecstatic, I asked when the job would open up.

"Mid-March," he responded.

At risk of suffering a heart attack, I finished covering the game, returned home, and told Brittney. We rejoiced like crazy—for a short while, anyway.

Because God nudged me again.

> Whoever knows the right thing to do and fails to do it, for
> him it is sin (James 4:17).

This time, I could swear he was telling me to quit my job before I heard whether or not I had been hired for the new job. And as humanly stupid as it was, that's exactly what I did.

I remember discussing James 4:17 with Brittney and talking about how I didn't want to quit, but felt so strongly that I knew it would be sin if I didn't. "That tells me this is from him," I said.

Looking back, I still shake my head. Not because it was a stupid move. But because it took me twenty-four years before I actually did something in complete faith—something that has radically changed the way I think of *impossible*. Not only did I get the job, but God unleashed a floodgate of blessings into our lives. The biggest blessing of all? Learning that risk-taking in good faith ultimately points to Jesus.

What do you think is too big for you? Things you have a conviction about but are too afraid to act on? It's never too early or too late to start taking risks for Jesus and learning what true security is. As a couple, clasp hands together and leap. Ask how you can challenge each other to live outside your comfort zones. To do things that require faith and force you to rely on God.

Exude Humility

I was never the popular kid growing up. Girls didn't line up to behold my looks, coo at my personality, or stand amazed at my athleticism. Pride wasn't my big problem. More like insecurity. I used to beat myself up constantly, telling myself there was no way on earth that a girl as amazing as Brittney would ever notice me, let alone like me.

But then…she did.

Sometimes I still ask her, "Why did you choose me?" I've asked her so many times, I can pretty much quote her response: "You were not loud and boisterous and egotistical. You made eye contact and actually asked questions and cared about the people in the room. You were a good listener, you respected authority, and you were humble—but at the same time, you weren't afraid to be a leader."

When you're in a relationship, a little voice constantly badgers you to look your best, sound your best, do your best. And while none of these things are wrong, the motives behind them can be.

So clothe yourself with humility. Our majestic King of Kings and Lord of Lords was born a baby on earth. He allowed sinners to raise him. And finally, he humbled himself to the lowliest, most despicable death of all—death on a cross.

How can you be humble in speech and in actions in your relationship? How can you decrease so that Jesus will increase? Don't seek the spotlight. Your other sees you just fine. Instead, point the spotlight to God and crush whatever pride exists in you.

Be Authentic

Like many, I've struggled my entire life with being authentic. There's something inside every human that fears being known—and this is especially true in relationships. Instead of saying what's really on our minds, we guess what our other wants to hear. Instead of doing what we believe is right, we try to figure out what our other thinks is right. We forsake authenticity because we fear that if we peel back the layers to the core of our true being, our other won't love us.

This must end if we want to point to Jesus. Embrace your authentic self. Not your sin, but your identity as a Christ-follower. Center your life on loving God with all of your heart and loving others in the same way you love yourself, "and all these things will be added to you" (Matthew 6:33).

Being authentic in what you say and how you act in your relationship is acceptance of who you are in Christ. It communicates to your other that, while you may not be totally happy with yourself, you trust that Jesus isn't finished with you yet.

Take Time to Pray

I have never, ever regretted taking the time to pray with Brittney. Focusing on God and opening our hearts together encourages us, empowers us, and brings us peace.

> Prayer pushes us in all the right directions.
>
> Paul David Tripp[2]

It's hard to explain, but after I pour out my heart and listen to Brittney pour out hers, a sort of realignment occurs—as if every link in our lives clinks back into place. Pride is swallowed. Hope is renewed. Purpose is rekindled.

Don't be embarrassed about talking with God in front of each other. Be bold, be empowered, and approach God's throne of grace with confidence so that you "may receive mercy and find grace to help in time of need" (Hebrews 4:16). Pray in a way that genuinely reflects how Jesus taught us to pray in Luke 11. Praise God, proclaim his beautiful will, ask for provision and protection from the enemy, and confess your sins.

Delight in Keeping God's Commandments

Whether it be a getaway trip, dinner out, a walk in the park, or something completely random, I love planning surprises for Brittney. But the best part isn't necessarily the surprise. It's the figurative stepping into her shoes and thinking about what will make her smile.

I delight in delighting her.

This is the attitude God wants us to have toward his commands. He doesn't want us begrudgingly obeying him because that's what Christians should do. He wants us to keep them joyfully because he loves us, knows what's best for us, and is pleased when his children obey.

You point to Jesus every time you live in joy and hope. You point to Jesus every time you overflow with love, peace, patience, kindness, goodness, and faithfulness in spite of the difficulties. You point to him when your heart is glad and when your whole being rejoices regardless of your circumstances.

Be someone who delights in doing God's will in your relationship. Instead of complaining about how hard flying can be, relish in the truth that your desire to love your other the way Jesus loves is a beautiful thing in the sight of God—and that he blesses obedience.

> For this is the love of God, that we keep his commandments. And his commandments are not burdensome (1 John 5:3).

Speak of Your Identity in Christ

It took a long time for Jesus to grab ahold of my heart, but when he did, my life flipped upside-down in a glorious way. The best part? Discovering my identity—and speaking of it freely and unashamedly.

Before then, insecurity ruled my life. I said what I thought others wanted to hear. I did things I thought others wanted me to do. I conformed to the image of the people around me.

But God snatched me up and changed all of that. He showed me that I was his son. A fellow heir of the kingdom. Holy and blameless because of Jesus. In short, he showed me who I was, and this freed me to speak and do things out of the overflow of Jesus inside me. This dramatically changed my relationship with Brittney and everyone else in my life. I now gush about Jesus. I thirst for the Word of God. I feel filled with the Holy Spirit.

If you've given your life to Jesus, he is your identity. No matter what life takes from you, you are still whole in him. No matter what adversity strikes, you still have a living hope. But does your other know this about you? Do you speak of Jesus and his utmost importance in your life? Does your life shout that you don't simply know *about* Christ, but truly know him and love him? Speaking openly of your identity in Christ helps you build your relationship on an unshakable foundation.

Concern Yourself with Motive

I'm always impressed when someone willingly gives you a glimpse into their inner motives—when they could have just as easily withheld it and looked better.

All through Scripture, we find that God is more interested in our motives than our actions. A great way to point to Jesus in your relationship is to openly concern yourself with the purpose behind your behavior. When you and your other pray, ask God to search your hearts, convict you of wrong motives, and stir you to do all things for his glory.

> The LORD said to Samuel, "Do not look on his appearance or on the height of his stature, because I have rejected him. For the LORD sees not as man sees: man looks on the outward appearance, but the LORD looks on the heart" (1 Samuel 16:7).

Tell Others About Jesus

The greatest leaps in my faith come from sharing my faith with others. In college, in the workplace, in evangelistic efforts. Something powerful happens when you express what you believe. It's a mysterious manifestation of Romans 10:17: "So faith comes from hearing, and hearing through the word of Christ."

When you tell others about Jesus, truth not only penetrates the hearers around you. It penetrates *you*. And in doing so, it increases your faith.

Think about what this means for your relationship. As you speak about Jesus in the presence of your other, you increase both your faith and your other's faith. You point everyone in earshot to Jesus. Remember that at family reunions, coffee shops, grocery stores, parties, community events, and really anywhere. Don't pass these moments up. They're awesome opportunities to point to the King, set a God-first tone in the relationship, and create great points of discussion for the two of you later on.

Serve Together

Putting the needs of others above your own is an awesome thing. I wish Brittney and I had done this more while dating. You learn a lot about yourself and your other when you serve God together.

But serving together isn't the first thing that pops into your mind when you think of a date. You'd prefer being exclusive, hanging out, eating together, and enjoying each other. But give it a try. Instead of going out to eat, go somewhere to serve others together. Instead of watching a movie, volunteer to watch the kids at your church while the parents go on a date. These things might seem trivial in the grand scheme, but they're vital. They set a precedent of sacrificial love in your relationship—which helps you go deeper than candles and romance and fun and games.

> For even the Son of Man came not to be served but to serve,
> and to give his life as a ransom for many (Mark 10:45).

Listen and Encourage

Each personality is different. Some people are outgoing, others are shy. Some are creative, others are logical. The list goes on. But no matter what, God makes it clear that your mindset should be to listen first, talk second, and radiate grace.

Do this in your relationship. Of course, don't count how many minutes you talk and how many minutes you listen. Instead, focus on quality listening and quality speaking. When your other is talking, really listen. Not just for what's being said on the surface, but underneath as well. And when you're speaking to your other, don't just speak because it's your turn. Do your best to formulate thoughts that add value to the conversation. For some this comes easy. For others it takes more effort. Regardless, make a concentrated effort to apply James 1:19: "Let every person be quick to hear, slow to speak, slow to anger."

Do Good to Haters

Chances are, at some point during the relationship one or both of you will come face-to-face with someone who treats you horribly. Maybe at work, maybe at a family gathering, maybe a disgruntled friend on social media.

The easy thing to do is rant about the other person's immaturity and hurtful actions. But Jesus doesn't call us to do the easy thing. He calls us to love and to do good to those who hate us. When tough situations like this arise, encourage your other to choose love. Discuss how you can "overcome evil with good" (Romans 12:21) and "do good to those who hate you" (Luke 6:27).

Consider Your Money as God's Money

I grew up with parents who valued frugality and discernment. They taught my brothers and me to spend wisely, save smartly, invest carefully, and give generously. Of these four financial aspects, the most difficult for me to embrace was giving.

God loves a cheerful giver (2 Corinthians 9:7). He tells us that it is more blessed to give than to receive (Acts 20:35). He also says give, and it will be given to you (Luke 6:38). In your relationship, set an example of generosity. Be the one who readily leaves tips, especially when they're not expected. Help out the person in line who has forgotten their wallet or purse. Contribute to projects that glorify Jesus, tithe more than you normally would, and pay for a homeless person's lunch. Also, when you hear that a friend is in need, cover the expense.

Treat your money like God's money, and listen for his nudging that it's time to use it for someone who will never pay you back. Consider keeping twenty dollars on you at all times to be used for no other purpose than blessing someone. In this, you point to Jesus.

Treat Other Believers as Fellow Heirs

My book *Called to Stay* discusses the messiness of church and challenges believers to be the change they long to see in their congregations. During the writing process, God strengthened my commitment to the Church and renewed my love for my brothers and sisters. But before then? I was bitter. I badmouthed. I let frustration turn to anger. I ignored God's command to love his children. My sin rendered me useless to Christ.

You and your other may be tempted to do the same. Some people may even tell you that your sin is justified—especially if your church is struggling right now.

But according to Jesus, we're never justified in bashing the Church. Take the high road. Discuss the qualities that your church excels in and talk of those things. Identify your spiritual gifts and practice them in your church, whether it be serving in the nursery, helping in the library, writing encouraging notes, tidying the pews, cooking meals, or making visitors feel welcome. Pray for your pastors and leaders and for those who are struggling with sin. When a conversation turns to gossip, boldly and humbly speak against it. As a couple, contribute to the solution, not to the problem.

Forgive Easily and Seek It Quickly

As your relationship evolves, your emotional connection will intensify, your talks will deepen, and the real you will be revealed. All this breathes life and energy into your relationship. But because we're sinners, conflict will inevitably rear its head. This isn't something to dread. If you handle conflict wisely and with intentionality, your relationship will actually be richer than if you never faced it at all.

We'd probably all love to have a conflict-free relationship, but there is nothing more reviving and unifying than resolving conflict with your other. And the key to conflict resolution is forgiveness, which can be broken down like this:

Be broken. Forgiveness isn't just about saying you're sorry. It arises out of a deep conviction and sorrow over how you've sinned against God and others. When you've done wrong in your relationship, what your other needs most is a sincere, broken you.

Be specific in your apologies. The more your words make you cringe, the closer you are to a true apology. There's a big difference between saying, "I'm sorry," and "I'm sorry for getting so angry, shutting you out, and acting like a child for the past two days. I have a lot of growing up to do. Would you forgive me?"

Be understanding. While God always will forgive you, unfortunately your other may not—at least, not right away. And you need to understand that and be okay with it. Regardless of how sorry you are, you cannot expect your apology to magically turn back the clock and undo your hurtful words or actions. Your other might need time to heal. Whether it takes a minute or a month, you must remain patient, humble, and repentant. Don't abuse the power of forgiveness by expecting it. Instead, pursue it as one who doesn't deserve it.

Seek refuge while you wait. Whether or not your other forgives you right away, hide in Christ. Spend time with him. Listen to him through the Holy Spirit. His loving eye is upon you, and he wants to teach you a better way. Let him purge all areas of sin from your life.

Always forgive. Jesus makes it clear that we must always, always forgive. Your other may sin against you in a way that ends or changes your relationship forever, but that does not exempt you from forgiving him or her like Jesus would.

Show compassion. God forgave our debt not with money, but by sacrificing his own precious son. We must remember this truth when we feel less than excited about extending forgiveness to our other. There is no sin so great that we cannot forgive. Show compassion and extend forgiveness in your relationship.

Forgive from your soul. It's not enough just to patch things up with your other and pretend everything is okay. It's only okay once you've forgiven from the deepest part of yourself. Don't bring up forgiven sin in bad taste. Don't use it as a weapon against your other at any time. Asking for forgiveness is a vulnerable thing. And if you pounce on that vulnerability, your other will build walls between you.

Write forgiveness letters to each other. You'd be surprised what will come out of you if you write it down. Sometimes our brains need more room to spill over what's in our hearts. Writing allows you to do this (and thankfully you can edit the words after they come out).

> Be kind to one another, tenderhearted, forgiving one another, as God in Christ forgave you (Ephesians 4:32).

Look Forward to Christ's Return

A shortcoming for many of us is our lukewarm attitude toward the return of Jesus and thrill of heaven—especially when we're in a relationship. Most of us at one point have longed for Jesus to stay put until we're married, had a family, and chased our dreams. We want to experience life and love with our other before the day of the Lord comes and eternity begins.

I'm not suggesting that you mechanically turn off your desire to marry your other. It would be foolish to tune out this wonderful longing. Instead, I'm suggesting that we all look forward to Christ's return and heaven in addition to our hopes for the relationship.

For instance, spend time thinking about finally meeting Jesus, the one who died on a tree in what some call the Great Exchange: all of your sin for

> Make heaven more real to me than any earthly thing has ever been.
>
> A.W. Tozer[3]
>
> Aim at heaven and you will get earth thrown in. Aim at earth and you get neither.
>
> C.S. Lewis[4]

all of his righteousness. What will you feel as his hand wipes away your tears? What will you do? What will you say?

Imagine what it will feel like to hear the words, "Well done, good and faithful servant" (Matthew 25:23), or discovering that your body has been made new and perfect. What emotion might spill out of you?

Picture entering a land like Eden, only better, built upon a mountain, surrounded by walls made of jasper and every kind of precious stone, with pearly gates that never shut. Imagine the immaculate roads and homes stretching fourteen hundred miles in each direction. What might it feel like to be in a place that's not only absent of sin and pain, but filled with the overwhelming presence of God?

Pondering a life beyond this earth requires the sweat of imagination. But doing so expands your view of God's majestic power, gives you more to praise and thank him for, spurs you on to live for him in every moment, and gives you hope and perspective when this life becomes laden with hardship.

In this deeper knowing and loving, you point to Jesus.

> They desire a better country, that is, a heavenly one. Therefore God is not ashamed to be called their God, for he has prepared for them a city (Hebrews 11:16).

Give Thanks in Good and Bad Times

Few feelings can compete with experiencing genuine love in a dating relationship. Even if I filled book after book, I wouldn't be able to recount all the wondrous moments I've shared with Brittney. Sometimes, I just gush thankfulness to God.

But there isn't one relationship on earth that sprouts roses without thorns. Hard stuff happens. Conflict with each other, conflict with family, work stress, financial problems...For most people, thankfulness to God disappears during these times. It's simply unnatural to pour out thanksgiving when difficulty arises. But here's the thing: Everything about living for Christ is unnatural—fighting against temptation, dying to self, loving our enemies. Rejoicing in trials is no different.

It's an indicator that Jesus matters more to you than this temporary life. It's a dead-giveaway opportunity to point to Jesus.

The next time difficulty rears its head in your relationship, thank God for the ways he may grow you through the pain. And when the hardship ends and you've had a chance to recover, discuss what God taught you.

> Count it all joy, my brothers, when you meet trials of various kinds, for you know that the testing of your faith produces steadfastness. And let steadfastness have its full effect, that you may be perfect and complete, lacking in nothing (James 1:2-4).

Approach Important Things Seriously

God knows everything about us—every selfish act, every hateful thought—and instead of casting us into the darkness, he invites us into his magnificent light to enjoy fellowship with him forever. It's mind-boggling. The Savior of the world wants to meet with us, no strings attached, no charge.

Yet how often do we rush through prayer, skim our Bible, or let our minds wander during worship, small group, communion, or the sermon?

We are children of God. We are friends of Jesus. But if we use these sweet truths to trump our need for deep awe and respect for our Creator, we steal glory due to him. We simply cannot lose the kind of heart David showed when he said, "What is mankind that you are mindful of them, human beings that you care for them?" (Psalm 8:4 NIV).

It's time that we reclaim reverence and joy before Jesus and point each other to him. Think of one way you can help stir up a greater reverence for God. Pray about it and discuss it with your other. Read Job 38 through 42 (and consider the context) to get a feel for the Almighty God we love and serve. Then talk with him like a child and ask him to help you see him and revere him for all that he is and all that he's done.

Discuss the Bible Together

Talking about regular life with your other is probably easy. Like, how you kind of accidentally blew a stoplight in front of a cop today, or how you dropped your phone in the toilet, or whether or not you want to go to that party. But the Bible? Not so easy. It takes intentionality, transparency, and starting before you're ready.

Be intentional. Set aside a specific time to spend in the Word together. Depending on your schedules, this might mean forgoing TV shows, game nights, or hanging out with friends.

Be transparent. The more transparent you are, the more profitable this time will be. If you struggle with a doctrinal idea, speak freely about it. If a passage convicts you to remove sin in your life, admit it. By setting a tone of transparency, you eliminate shallow conversation. The goal of this time is not to wow your other with theological knowledge or your ability to unearth deep spiritual nuggets. It's to grow in unity, share your innermost thoughts, offer insight, pray for each other's weaknesses, and discover God through his Word.

Start before you're ready. Don't wait until basketball season is over, or until you're done with a rigorous semester, or until your sister's wedding is over. Start today. The longer you wait to set aside time to discuss the Word together, the harder it will be to make it a priority in your relationship.

Don't worry about not having anything to say. The Bible is the most intricate book ever written. It bursts with beautiful complexity, allegorical stories, practical wisdom, mindboggling paradoxes, breathtaking miracles, powerful parables, and prophecy fulfilled. Woven through each page we see the weight of our sin and the greatness of our Savior's sacrifice. The issue isn't what to talk about. It's where to begin. Just pick a passage and dive in. The words will come.

As you read, differences in opinion will come up. You and your other don't need to agree on every doctrinal statement, possess the same measure of faith, or embrace identical biblical convictions. But you do need to be mindful of each other's differing opinions and wisely discern what is just a differing opinion and what is a deal breaker. This could result in some uncomfortable talks, but if you don't discuss these things now, you could be in for a very unwelcoming wake-up call later on.

So talk. Don't look to conform your other to your own personal views. Instead, see if any issues are honestly deal breakers.

Surround Yourself with Truth

A tribal chief once described his inner spiritual battle like a fight between a white wolf and a black wolf. When asked which wolf wins, he replied, "The one I feed the most."

Filling your relationship with wholesomeness—that is, feeding the white wolf—makes you strong. You don't need to be legalistic about it, but find practical ways to surround yourself and your other with truth.

For instance, listen to good music. Every day on my commute to the university, I cranked my favorite music that lifted up Jesus. And I was astounded by my immediate shift in perspective. Instead of getting swayed by the worldly views or the Christ-hating atmosphere, the lyrics infused my world with hope and reminded me of my identity in Jesus and purpose in life. Consider this in your relationship. Music can play a vital role. Jesus is everywhere, and music can be a beautiful reminder of that.

In addition, watch quality television. TV is designed to entertain you, and there is nothing wrong with that. Brittney and I love watching crime and comedy shows. But also consider watching something that produces spiritual discussion. There are plenty of solid videos out there that won't bore you to tears.

Pointing to Jesus Is the Most Attractive Thing About You

"Caleb, Brittney loves and is attracted to the Jesus in you," a mentor once told me.

That idea, though so simple, clarified everything in my mind. Brittney didn't love me for just being Caleb. At the core, she loved me for the small ways that I pointed her to Jesus—for giving her what she needed most instead of taking what I wanted now.

If your other truly loves Christ, he or she will love and be attracted to how you point to Jesus—not just your ability to whip up a nice dinner date. Never succumb to what the world says you need in order to attract someone and enjoy an amazing relationship. It's just not true. Don't make it your goal to look sexy and find perfect romance. It doesn't exist—not in the sense the world looks at it, anyway. Perfect romance only exists in Jesus, who "while we were still sinners…died for us" (Romans 5:8). Point to that kind of love and you will attract someone for the right reason. The beautiful reason.

Don't settle for just pointing at the fact that you're a good person, with good intentions, who really wants to invest your life into a good relationship.

Settle for nothing less than what you and your other need most.

What's Next

We've looked at the core of what it means to give your other what's needed most. Now let's look at some practical *dos* and *don'ts* of a flying relationship.

Ask Those Who Fly

In what ways did you point your other to Jesus?

Serving together was one way we pointed each other to Jesus and kept the relationship focused on living for him. We especially enjoyed getting involved with evangelistic out-reach opportunities with our church. We would go out together to a college campus or the mall and talk to strangers about how to be saved. Working together to spread the gospel was a great way to encourage each other in our walks with the Lord.

Andrew & Abigail

As our relationship grew, we were both pointed to Jesus as we learned how to get over ourselves and put the other's needs above ours. We had to humble ourselves to learn how to communicate best. I realized I struggled with holding grudges and being bitter. I had to spend a lot of time praying, asking Jesus to soften my heart, and show me how to truly love Jake.

Sarah

In what ways did your other point *you* to Jesus?

I have recently been struggling with depression. Cody knows when I'm lying to myself and reminds me what's true. He tells me it's okay to feel sad, encourages me to do things that bring me joy, and reminds me that everything is good because of Jesus.

Kaisha

Kristi has a constant faith and devotion to Jesus. He is central to her view of life and circumstances. She is zealous to have Christ as the center of her life. As such, she brought her worship of Christ into our relationship.

Josh

Jessi showed me Jesus by teaching me a different kind of love—how to love the seemingly unlovable. She's compassionate when I would tend to be dismissive or judgmental, and God used her example to change that in me. She also exhibited devotion and true constancy.

Matt

Jen had a longing for truth and a passion for Jesus that I wanted. There was freshness to her relationship with Christ that was evident—and it was contagious! She couldn't get enough of Christ, and it encouraged me in my walk.

Aaron

Heather sends me texts with Scripture quotes throughout the day. She lets me know how she's been praying for me. She shares insights about God. And she does this thing that I really recommend: She asks herself, "How has God been good to me today?" She asks me as well, and it has blessed me so much to focus on where I see God throughout the day instead of focusing on the negative and becoming bitter.

Jeff

Jeff points me to Jesus in the way he displays Christ's character. He's humble enough to recognize that he's not always right. If there's a perceived wrong, Jeff responds really quickly. He can sense the conviction of God. Jeff also encourages me to see things from a different perspective that has helped me be less judgmental. He's broadened my perspective without compromising the truth of the gospel.

Heather

What difficulties did you face in pointing each other to Jesus?

I think we all like to think we have all the answers. It's not all that fun to realize our need for help, but being in a relationship reveals that like no other time. It is very humbling.

Jake & Sarah

Thinking, speaking, and acting from our old flesh has been the foremost obstacle to pointing one another to Jesus. Sometimes I get offended by something Kristi does, hold a grudge, and keep her at arm's length emotionally.

Josh

We are and were both very aggressive people, and as former athletes, we both wanted to win. It is hard to lose an argument when the other person is just as competitive as you are. That was a definite struggle for us.

Aaron

 Did your relationship ever open opportunities to tell others about Jesus?

We definitely hope that in a world with so much divorce, betrayal, and broken relationships, simply living a good marriage will be proof of Jesus to others. I think that with time, the testimony of Jesus in our marriage will become stronger.

Kaisha

We remained pure, choosing not to live together until we were married. This was very different from the norm, and it presented us with opportunities to share with our unbelieving friends why we made those choices and what the commitment of marriage means to us.

Jake & Sarah

Throughout our courtship, Isaac considered it a blessing to be able to show his coworkers and college classmates that a godly relationship can be lasting, fulfilling, and good. In the face of the pessimism of many, we both tried to live out God's love to one another in hopes of letting others see God's light, love, and blessing in us.

Melissa

Jen's family is not saved and they have started reading their Bibles and being interested in what we believe. We've seen fruit from our marriage even with close family.

Aaron

Part 3

FLYING

10

DOS AND DON'TS

Are you putting yourself in situations where you can be
pursued? Are you in a place where you can be noticed? Can
you do anything to put yourself in somebody's mind-set?

GARY THOMAS

Do Look for Someone

God knows the plans he has for you. But he's also given you the freedom to pursue options, take actions, and make decisions. The message throughout the entire Bible is that God knows, but you must go.

If you are in search of that special someone, don't sit back and continue the same old routine as though God hasn't called you to action. Likewise, if you're searching like crazy for that special someone without success, don't sweat and moan as though God isn't in control or doesn't know what's best for you.

Search for someone as you would a career. Work on making yourself the best candidate, apply and interview to the best of your ability—and, at the end of the day, see if someone responds.

Become the Best Candidate

This is what this book is all about. It's why so many pages are dedicated to your relationship with Jesus. You simply cannot be the best candidate for another believer if you are not head-over-heels in love with Christ and following his commands.

Apply and Interview

Get yourself out there. If no one in your life is marriage material, find places to meet new people. If you're already interested in someone, find ways to pursue a friendship. Don't cling. Don't show off. Just aim to be yourself in a setting where he or she is present. Put yourself on their radar. Be discoverable. And if a conversation arises, ask good questions, be an attentive listener, and above all, strive for your words, actions, and motives to point to Jesus.

When the conversation is over—and if you feel it's appropriate—tell them how much you enjoyed yourself and that you hope to see them again. Be subtle enough to be proper, but forward enough to convey the message that you're interested.

See If Someone Responds

If you're pursuing Jesus and placing yourself in situations where God can work, you've done your part. At some point, the other needs to respond. Sometimes the response is *no*. Sometimes it's *not yet*. And sometimes it's that amazing *yes*.

Don't Think a Relationship Will Cure Your Sin Issues

It won't. If you struggle with lust, addiction, anger, pride, laziness, or countless other sins, getting into a relationship isn't going to fix that problem. In fact, it might amplify certain sins or reveal new ones you hadn't previously struggled with.

If you really want to give your other what he or she needs most over taking what you want now, you need to do what it takes to purge the predominant sins in your life right now. I understand this is easier said than done. That's why you need a strategy. A game plan.

I suggest you do three things.

Be honest with yourself. Look at your life, examine your heart, and pinpoint the areas that are riddled with sin. It's imperative that you stop lying to yourself. Don't soften your sin with excuses or by comparing yourself to others. Instead, try to see your sin the way God sees it.

Recruit accountability. Ask someone you respect and trust to question you about the areas in your life you'd rather keep secret. Give them permission to ask you hard questions and speak openly about sin patterns they've seen in your life.

Take drastic action. If you struggle with lust, break your phone or computer. If you struggle with debt, chop up your credit cards. Get help from a brother or sister in Christ. You simply cannot give your other what he or she needs most if you're wallowing in sin. Ask Jesus to help you. He will.

Often, there are many things you need to work on before you're ready to marry. Sometimes there are habitual sins, such as porn addiction, that need to be addressed. Other times, you need to work on establishing yourself to be in a position to provide for a family or grow stronger in your spiritual life.

Mark Driscoll[1]

I would be lying if I told you this process is easy. But the rewards are limitless. Remember, flying will initially be harder than falling. But falling will always pale in comparison to the true freedom of flying.

Do Talk About Roles Within Marriage

I grew up in a traditional home. My dad worked full-time at the family car business and my mom stayed home caring for my brothers and me. She cooked amazing meals and kept our house looking like a palace. My dad came home in the evenings, ate dinner with the family, mowed the lawn, and fixed things that needed fixing. Each of them took up a role and embraced it wholeheartedly. They were—and are— the perfect team.

For your grandparents there was little, if any, disagreement on gender roles, but it's now become controversial. The problem is, while gender roles within church and marriage are discussed thoroughly in seminaries, few dating couples are aware of this issue and fewer still discuss it.

Gary Thomas[2]

My marriage with Brittney looks much different. From the day we got married, we wanted to pursue careers in writing. This endeavor was anything but traditional. In the beginning I worked as a sports journalist, which gave Brittney the freedom to write. Years later, I quit my job to write full-time and she took a part-time job at our church. Then we took a night manager position at a retirement home, which allowed both of us to write for several hours each week.

The point is this: God doesn't create cookie-cutter people who live cookie-cutter lives. Every marriage is different. What matters is whether you and your other agree on what Scripture says about marital roles. I encourage you to study passages that deal with this topic specifically. Ask deep questions and seek counsel.

If you discover that you both drastically disagree, consider it a major red flag. It might not seem like a big deal now, but once the reality of marriage hits, your roles will come alive in a very beautiful—or very monstrous—way.

Consider Jace and Elizabeth. On the surface they were made for each other. Their relationship was going strong: dating with an eye toward marriage, followers of Jesus, the whole bit. They even started eyeing rings.

Then they talked about roles in marriage.

Jace pretty much deadpanned that men shouldn't change diapers, do dishes, or cook. He even went so far as to use Scripture to justify his points. The relationship didn't last much beyond that conversation.

If two people are on board with the roles each might fulfill in marriage, great. But if your other starts dropping *shouldn'ts*, you need to take that seriously. It means the other is unlikely to change his or her mind.

I like grocery shopping more than Brittney does, and she likes washing the car more than I do. This doesn't mean I do all the shopping, nor does it mean she always washes the car. It simply means we're in agreement on things that might seem backward to others. We don't think pushing a shopping cart, cooking, or changing diapers emasculates me or my leadership. And we also don't think washing the car, mowing the lawn, or having an opinion defeminizes Brittney.

Obviously, roles in marriage is a discussion you'll only want to bring up if your relationship is for sure moving toward marriage. Bringing up gender roles on your first date isn't exactly a recipe for a budding relationship. But if you're far enough along that you believe rings and a wedding are on the horizon, address this issue. It's more important than most people think and will affect the entire scope of your lives together.

Don't Think You Have to Date Around to Find the Right Person

If I got a quarter for every time someone told me this, I could've bought a new phone. It didn't matter that Brittney and I were in love and wanted to get married. People simply thought I needed to experience multiple relationships before I ever considered marriage. "You wouldn't run a marathon without training for it, would you?" they'd say.

No. That would be silly. But you wouldn't cut off chunks of your running shoes either. Yet that's exactly what people do when they date and break up, date and break up.

You don't need to date a bunch of people to prepare for marriage. You need to love Jesus, mature in your faith, and walk humbly with your God.

Do Take the Relationship Slow

No potential buyer ever walks into a house for the first time, glances around, and says, "I'll take it." And it would strike you as odd if a student took a single day

> The Bible doesn't give us an "oops, I acted too hastily" clause when it comes to marriage and divorce.
>
> Gary Thomas[3]

to decide which college to attend. The bigger the decision, the more time we take to make it

But the rush of falling in love makes you feel so weightless, so empowered, so free that it's easy to act impulsively. *More, more, more—faster, faster, faster.*

Choose to pace yourself. Practice patience. You and your other need to spend a good amount of time together before deciding on forever.

Is it wrong to rush to the altar? Not always. The issue isn't about days or weeks or months. It's about wisdom, discernment, and maturity. If you and your other are confident in these things—and others support you in this decision, preferably—then now is the time.

Do Look for Someone Who's Attracted to the Jesus in You

I'll be the first to admit that my wife was way out of my league.

I fell in love with Brittney the moment I met her. Her smile lit up my world, her exuberant personality filled a room, and the way her ears poked out of her hair was too cute to describe. She was a dream I didn't want to wake up from.

But I had no business liking her. There were so many other guys who were more attractive, more athletic, smarter, funnier, better. Oh, and one more thing. She was taller than me. Yeah. She was way out of my league.

Or so I thought.

Brittney fell in love with me because she saw Jesus in me.

It's more important to radiate the character of Jesus than to have rock-hard abs, name-brand clothes, a well-paying job, a fancy car, a bunch of friends, or a high IQ. There is certainly nothing wrong with these things, but they shouldn't define your worth. Instead, be like Jesus and the right people will notice.

Likewise, don't look for someone who fulfills a checklist of external qualities. Though things like physical attraction, parallel goals, and complementary personalities are important, they shouldn't trump the most important quality: a relationship with Jesus.

Don't Believe There Is Only One Special Person for You

> The language of the Bible doesn't suggest there is one right choice for marriage. Rather, all the teaching passages seem to suggest that there are wise and unwise choices. We are encouraged to use wisdom, not destiny, as our guide when choosing a marital partner.
>
> Gary Thomas[4]

The world sells us the whimsical idea that if you just keep searching, eventually you will find your soul mate, the one person in all of creation who will fill your heart with joy, dry your every tear, and hang on your every word.

This is a lie.

Great relationships don't happen when you find your "soul mate." They happen when you find someone who shares your desire to fly, who wants to point to Jesus in all things, who chooses to give what's needed most over what's wanted now.

And this is great news.

If it were true that there were only one perfect person for you, it would be easy to question whether or not you found the right person when things got rough. In fact, you might even use this logic to justify ending a relationship and moving on to the next person you think is "the one." This is how many people date today, always looking for the one, always hitting a snag in the relationship, and always moving on to the next person.

If you subscribe to the idea of *the one*, let it go. Instead focus on being the one.

Do Pray for the Right Person

Finding the right person to spend the rest of your life with is one of the biggest decisions you'll ever make, yet very few people pray about it.

Whether we admit it or not, prayer can often seem like a fanciful notion that yields no results. I'm sure we're all guilty of uttering a prayer, waiting a week, and thinking, "Well, that didn't work. God must not care."

But prayer doesn't operate like an ATM. You can't swipe a prayer card and instantly receive a bundle of answers. Yet God instructs us to pray. He tells us he hears the cry of the righteous and says if his words remain in us that we may ask any request we like—and it will be granted according to *his* will. He says "the prayer of a righteous person has great power as it is working" (James 5:16).

So make your requests known to him. Be brave. Be bold. Be honest. Bear your soul like you never have before. God's eyes are on those who humble themselves enough to talk with him as a child talks to his daddy. Ask him to help you become the right person for your future other. Ask him to stir his Spirit inside you to conquer your fear, give you the words to say when you're nervous, and move you to be in the right places at the right times.

Get real with God and don't shy away from going to him again and again as you search for your special other.

What's Next

If you're ready for something better than falling, something that rises to the transcendence of Jesus, then it's time for you to fly.

Ask Those Who Fly

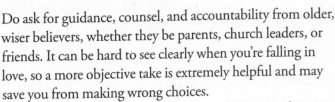

What dos and don'ts would you suggest to those interested in starting a relationship?

Do ask for guidance, counsel, and accountability from older, wiser believers, whether they be parents, church leaders, or friends. It can be hard to see clearly when you're falling in love, so a more objective take is extremely helpful and may save you from making wrong choices.

Andrew & Abigail

Don't be afraid of relationship "failure." For years I thought that because the end goal of dating was marriage, a breakup meant a failed relationship. But in reality, the end goal of dating is to find out if marriage is an option. If a couple realizes marriage is not going to work for them and break it off, the relationship was successful. If they decide marriage is a great idea and proceed that way, the relationship was successful. Beginning to date someone is a scary thing, and I think it takes a lot of pressure off to realize that a breakup, although hard, is not the end of the world or a failure.

Kaisha

Do spend as much time getting to know each other as friends before beginning a relationship. Spend time together in groups of friends where you are both comfortable. You'll get to know each other better because you'll both be as close to "yourself" as possible. It will also give you a chance to learn if you're compatible or have similar interests before being involved romantically.

Jake & Sarah

Don't get close physically without first getting even closer spiritually. Do find ways to express your love and appreciation for him or her verbally before anything else.

Corina

Don't neglect to serve together. We participated in the same short-term mission trip, volunteered our time at church, and served as a couple in lay ministry. This helped us to realize that God's role for us went beyond our relationship; it was about serving the church and loving people.

Matt

Do read a book about God together. It makes God the center of the relationship and springs conversations about spiritual things which might not otherwise be brought up. Don't assume that God will come into your relationship later by accident. Within the first few weeks of our relationship, we read *Knowing God* together and had incredibly deep conversations! We grew to appreciate each other's spiritual walk with the Lord early on, which provided security and direction for the rest of our relationship.

Kyle

Don't get into a relationship unless marriage is possible in the near future and that is your intent. What I mean is that if you're starting a relationship and it will be three years before you graduate college and find a job or even graduate high school for that matter, it might be best to wait until marriage can happen without having to date for years and years. Long-term dating is difficult. The more you fall in love with and are looking forward to marrying the person, the harder purity gets. Now to clarify, I am not saying that you have to necessarily graduate college and have all your ducks in a row in order to get married.

But I think couples who date long-term would tell you it isn't the best option.

Bailey

Do take some time to observe before making your feelings known. Infatuation is a strong, compulsive feeling, kind of like temporary insanity. You will do anything for the other person, even things that you absolutely hate. In my experience, I wasn't doing things because I loved Heather. I was doing it because I loved the attention I was getting and loved the feeling that came with that. If you jump right into a relationship early on in infatuation, then you will likely see the other person through rose-colored glasses. They can do no wrong. You may mistake infatuation for love. So go do stuff with a group of some mutual friends. Take a season or two to see if your feelings grow or fade. It's a lot easier to realize you don't like someone when you are not dating them.

Jeff

Do spend a lot of time in prayer. If your intention of dating is to ultimately get married, it's really important to make sure you do your best to be aligned with the Lord's will. He will bring clarity and peace if pursuing a relationship is the right path for you.

Jake & Sarah

Don't rush the dating process. We wanted to see each other in life's best and worst situations. We wanted to discern character and see what the other person was really like. That kind of insight comes through years of investing in someone else's life.

Matt

Do invest time and resources toward winning the heart of your potential spouse's family. You're becoming a part of his or her entire family. Pursue them too! Don't allow a "me vs. your family" attitude to form. When you marry, you've permanently joined your spouse's family and have a keen interest in its success. Enjoy the new family you've been adopted into. Forgive real or perceived slights or cultural and lifestyle differences.

Josh

Don't go overboard on how you are going to make your intentions known. One of my good friends was going to spend some time with a female with the goal of expressing to her his feelings. And his plan was to express these feelings in a poem. Now I'm sure most of the ladies are swooning at the thought of their dream guy doing something like this, and at face value it is really sweet...but what if she wasn't interested? That is a lot of emotional energy to invest into asking her if you could go on a couple of dates. On top of that, I think that this had as much potential of just feeling awkward for the girl as it did of sweeping her off of her feet. Simply go out for a cup of coffee, tell her how you feel, and let her express how she feels and then maybe schedule the first date.

Jeff

Do communicate right away about the purpose of the relationship. The purpose of dating is to find a marriage partner. But not everyone is ready for that. One person may have the idea of engagement and marriage as soon as possible. Someone else may be thinking marriage after I finish my four-year degree. Both people need to have the same end goal for the relationship.

Kaisha

Don't be afraid to ask questions that you feel are important. This may lead to the end of any possible romantic relationships, but it's better to find out early than to wait until you're emotionally invested.

Jake & Sarah

Do pray for one another, both together and individually. My wife's childhood and young adult years were tougher than mine, so we prayed through them together. We also prayed about the future (college, marriage, careers). One of the most helpful things, however, was when we prayed for other people. By collectively shifting our attention to the needs of others, we were able to see God's goodness in our relationship more clearly.

Matt

Don't have unrealistic expectations. We need to be aware that we are human. I've met girls who are only willing to accept someone who is flawless. Or they've compared themselves with older married couples whose healthy relationship is the result of hard work and commitment. You're not going to find someone like that right away.

Heather

Do take your time in the relationship! So many people act like there's some sort of rush to start dating, get engaged, and get married. I think a lot of that comes from pressure from those around us. We ask questions like, "So, is it official yet?" and "He hasn't proposed yet?" We can get left feeling pressured into rushing things. Go with the timing that's best for you. Kyle and I were good friends for two years before we started dating. I'm so thankful that we went into our relationship as best friends. It resulted in a great foundation for lives together.

Tayler

Don't think that "taking the next step" will help improve dysfunction within the relationship. Issues need to be settled before pursuing the next step in a relationship. If they are not being resolved, it might be an indication that the relationship shouldn't continue.

Jake & Sarah

Don't expect your other to change and don't make them into a project. If you don't think you could marry a person as is, if you are thinking of marrying a person with an idea of them being more to your liking in the future, you've got a serious warning sign. I think it's more helpful to ask a question like, *Am I okay with the prospect that they will not change in this arena? If the car was always dirty, if they remain a spender rather than a saver, if they don't become a better listener, would I still want to be with them or will that just drive me nuts?*

Jeff

11

FLY

*Love with God's love... Walk out the gospel on a daily
basis, forgiving, serving, and putting others first.*

GARY THOMAS

Flying isn't just a Christian way to date. It's simply practicing
true love—Jesus love—in your relationship.

When you choose to fly, you are showing Christ to the world and
inviting people everywhere to explore the source of true love. You are
using one more avenue for the planting of seeds and, ultimately, the
fulfillment of your paramount purpose: to make followers of Jesus.

If you choose to fly—to get up and dance when everyone else is sitting on the hillside—you are choosing to infuse every part of your life
and romance with true, powerful, authentic, sacrificial Jesus love.

Will it be difficult? It's the hardest thing you'll ever do.

Will you fail? Count on it.

Will Jesus be with you? Every second of every day.

The choice is yours.

Will you fall?

Or *fly?*

How priceless is your unfailing love, O God!
People take refuge in the shadow of your wings.

—Psalm 36:7 (NIV)

NOTES

Chapter 1

1. Gary Thomas, *The Sacred Search* (Colorado Springs, CO: David C. Cook, 2013), Kindle edition, chap. 2.
2. Ibid., chap. 18.
3. A.W. Tozer, *The Pursuit of God* (Christian Miracle Foundation Press, 2011), Kindle edition, chap. 3.
4. Rebecca St. James, *Wait for Me* (Nashville, TN: Thomas Nelson, 2008), Kindle edition, chap. 5.
5. Paul David Tripp, *What Did You Expect?* (Wheaton, IL: Good News Publishers, 2010), Kindle edition, chap. 12.
6. Thomas, *The Sacred Search*, chap. 11.

Chapter 3

1. Henry Cloud and John Townsend, *Boundaries in Dating* (Grand Rapids, MI: Zondervan, 2009), Kindle edition, chap. 3.
2. Rebecca St. James, *Wait for Me* (Nashville, TN: Thomas Nelson, 2008), Kindle edition, chap. 5.
3. Mark Driscoll, "Dating, Relating, and Fornicating," pastormark.tv, October 26, 2011, http://pastormark.tv/2011/10/26/dating-relating-and-fornicating.
4. A.W. Tozer, *The Pursuit of God* (Christian Miracle Foundation Press, 2011), Kindle edition, chap. 1.
5. Cloud and Townsend, *Boundaries in Dating*, chap. 3.
6. Paul David Tripp, *What Did You Expect?* (Wheaton, IL: Good News Publishers, 2010), Kindle edition, chap. 12.
7. Gary Thomas, *The Sacred Search* (Colorado Springs, CO: David C. Cook, 2013), Kindle edition, chap. 5.
8. Ibid., chap. 18.
9. Driscoll, "Dating, Relating, and Fornicating."
10. Dannah Gresh, *What Are You Waiting For?* (Doubleday Religious Publishing Group), Kindle edition, chap. 4.
11. Cloud and Townsend, *Boundaries in Dating*, chap. 17.
12. Thomas, *The Sacred Search*, chap. 2.
13. Driscoll, "Dating, Relating, and Fornicating."
14. Thomas, *The Sacred Search*, chap. 5.

Chapter 4

1. Henry Cloud and John Townsend, *Boundaries in Dating* (Grand Rapids, MI: Zondervan, 2009), Kindle edition, chap. 2.

2. Gary Thomas, *The Sacred Search* (Colorado Springs, CO: David C. Cook, 2013), Kindle edition, chap. 4.

3. Isaac Hydoski, "A Pastoral Response to Online Dating," joshharris.com, May 17, 2007, http://www.joshharris.com/2007/05/a_pastoral_response_to_online.php

4. Thomas, *The Sacred Search*, chap. 4.

5. Mark Driscoll, "Dating, Relating, and Fornicating," pastormark.tv, October 26, 2011, http://pastormark.tv/2011/10/26/dating-relating-and-fornicating.

Chapter 5

1. A.W. Tozer, *The Pursuit of God* (Christian Miracle Foundation Press, 2011), Kindle edition, preface.

2. Laura Smit, *Loves Me, Loves Me Not* (Grand Rapids, MI: Baker Academic & Brazos Press, 2005), Kindle edition, chap. 5.

3. Tozer, *The Pursuit of God*, chap. 3.

4. Augustine, *Confessions*, trans. Henry Chadwick, (New York: Oxford University Press, 1991), 3.

Chapter 6

1. Henry Cloud and John Townsend, *Boundaries in Dating* (Grand Rapids, MI: Zondervan, 2009), Kindle edition, chap. 7.

2. Shaunti Feldhahn, *For Women Only* (Sisters, OR: Multnomah, 2004), Kindle edition, chap. 6.

3. Cloud and Townsend, *Boundaries in Dating*, chap. 17.

4. Dannah Gresh, *What Are You Waiting For?* (Doubleday Religious Publishing Group), Kindle edition, chap. 6.

5. Rebecca St. James, *Wait for Me* (Nashville, TN: Thomas Nelson, 2008), Kindle edition, chap. 3.

6. "Sexual and Reproductive Health of Persons Aged 10-24 Years," July 17, 2009, http://www.cdc.gov/mmwr/preview/mmwrhtml/ss5806a1.htm?s_cid=ss5806a1_e#tab2.

7. Tyler McKenzie, "How I Know My Wife Married the Wrong Person (Part 4)," crossshapedstuff.com, http://crossshapedstuff.com/2013/06/17/how-i-know-my-wife-married-the-wrong-person-part-4/.

8. Brandon Andersen, "5 Notes on Dating for the Guys," theresurgence.com, http://theresurgence.com/2012/08/28/5-notes-on-dating-for-the-guys.

9. H. Norman Wright, *101 Questions to Ask Before You Get Engaged* (Eugene, OR: Harvest House Publishers, 2004), Kindle edition, chap. 2.

10. Gresh, *What Are You Waiting For?*, chap. 5.

11. Ibid.

12. Mark Driscoll, "Dating, Relating, and Fornicating," pastormark.tv, October 26, 2011, http://pastormark.tv/2011/10/26/dating-relating-and-fornicating.

13. Andersen, "5 Notes on Dating for the Guys."

Chapter 7

1. Henry Cloud and John Townsend, *Boundaries in Dating* (Grand Rapids, MI: Zondervan, 2009), Kindle edition, chap. 3.

2. Gary Thomas, *The Sacred Search* (Colorado Springs, CO: David C. Cook, 2013), Kindle edition, chap. 13.

3. Jack and Carole Mayhall, *Marriage Takes More Than Love* (Colorado Springs, CO: NavPress, 1978), 38-39.

4. Paul David Tripp, *What Did You Expect?* (Wheaton, IL: Good News Publishers, 2010), Kindle edition, chap. 11.

Chapter 8

1. Gary Thomas, *The Sacred Search* (Colorado Springs, CO: David C. Cook, 2013), Kindle edition, chap. 9.

2. H. Norman Wright, *101 Questions to Ask Before You Get Engaged* (Eugene, OR: Harvest House Publishers, 2004), Kindle edition, chap. 2.

3. Thomas, *The Sacred Search,* chap. 9.

4. Wright, *101 Questions to Ask Before You Get Engaged,* chap. 1.

5. Joshua Harris, *Boy Meets Girl* (Colorado Springs, CO: Multnomah, 2005), 102.

Chapter 9

1. Mark Driscoll, "Dating, Relating, and Fornicating," pastormark.tv, October 6, 2011, http://pastormark.tv/2011/10/26/dating-relating-and-fornicating.

2. Paul David Tripp, *What Did You Expect?* (Wheaton, IL: Good News Publishers, 2010), Kindle edition, chap. 16.

3. A.W. Tozer, *The Pursuit of God* (Christian Miracle Foundation Press, 2011), Kindle edition, chap. 4.

4. C.S. Lewis, *Mere Christianity* (New York: HarperCollins, 1952), 135.

Chapter 10

1. Mark Driscoll, "Dating, Relating, and Fornicating," pastormark.tv, October 26, 2011, http://pastormark.tv/2011/10/26/dating-relating-and-fornicating.

2. Gary Thomas, *The Sacred Search* (Colorado Springs, CO: David C. Cook, 2013), Kindle edition, chap. 12.

3. Ibid., chap. 3.

4. Ibid., chap. 5.

Caleb Breakey is a former journalist and author of *Called to Stay*. Caleb is a frequent conference speaker with a sincere passion to lead, challenge, and inspire others in discussions about relationships, the church, and radically following Jesus. He lives in Washington State with his wife, Brittney.

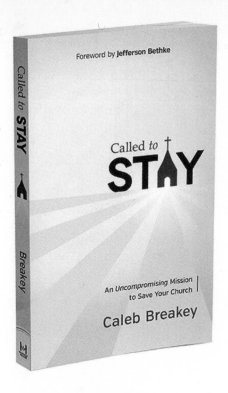

Will You Stay?
Caleb Breakey prays to God you do.

In *Called to Stay* Breakey takes a refreshingly honest look at the church, the problem of Millennials leaving, and the stark reality of why the church desperately needs them. He holds nothing back as he unleashes an ambitious rallying cry to heal the church and inject his generation's desire for truth, passion, and conviction into other believers.

Caleb knows that answering the challenge of his own generation leads to a transformed church.

And a changed church can change the world.